Praise for *Equitable Grading Unlocked*

Equitable Grading Unlocked captures the real struggle educators face with student assessment, grounding the work in teacher voice and best practice while providing a hopeful path forward. Each chapter invites meaningful dialogue and offers practical next steps that make change feel manageable and possible. From rubrics and retakes to gradebooks and late work, the book is anchored in reflective questions that echo those I've wrestled with throughout my career. A powerful theme throughout is authentically involving students in the assessment process, shifting assessment from something done to students to something experienced with them. As a teacher, I wish I would have had this book to guide my practice. As a leader at the school and district level, I see it as an invaluable resource to spark collaborative discussion and shared engagement among staff, creating the conditions for schoolwide growth. Its structure—spotlights, reflective questions, and practical next steps—makes it accessible and actionable for educators at every level.

—Jeff Snell
Executive Director, Washington Association of School Administrators

As educators, we all want grading practices that enhance learning and support and encourage all students in their education journeys, yet we're often stuck with systems from a bygone area designed to separate the wheat from the chaff—ensuring that some kids will be on the losing end of the equation. We know these systems aren't working for many of our students, but it's so hard to shift entrenched practices. Thanks to Howard and Maika, we now have a tool to do just that. *Equitable Grading Unlocked* is a powerful and *practical* guide for educators. Backed by clear and compelling evidence and supported by the work of real teachers in real classrooms, this book will help educators work toward having both high academic standards and grading practices that support all learners equitably."

—Mike Anderson
Award-winning teacher, national consultant
Bestselling author of *What We Say and How We Say It Matter*

Although discussions about grading have always been present in education, a recent and well-deserved focus has been put on ensuring that grading practices tell an accurate and equitable story of what a student knows and is able to do. What *Equitable Grading Unlocked* does that sets it apart from other resources is it provides a bridge that takes us from how we have traditionally—and inequitably—graded students to a better way of knowing and doing. At its core, this is a book for practitioners: teachers in the classroom and building leaders moving systems forward. The practical applications and thoughtful questions that come from those closest to the classroom make this book an essential companion to the compelling research that demands a change.

—**Greg Harris**
Principal, Adrienne C. Nelson High School
2019 Oregon Middle School Principal of the Year

Equitable Grading Unlocked is a transformative guide that masterfully bridges theory with practice in educational assessment. This groundbreaking work provides educators with concrete, actionable strategies to decouple practice from grading, ensuring that formative assessment truly serves learning rather than punishment. What sets this book apart is its compassionate yet practical handling of complex issues. This is an essential resource for any educator committed to creating truly equitable classrooms. This book doesn't just critique traditional grading; it provides the road map for meaningful change.

—**Starr Sackstein**
Massachusetts state coordinator for Educators Rising
COO of Mastery Portfolio
Author of *Student-Led Assessment*

This is no one-size-fits-all book about grading. Implementing equitable grading practices is a deeply personal and unique journey for each teacher. Howard Yank and Maika Yeigh unpack the most challenging aspects of equitable grading in a format that makes it easy for teachers to choose where to begin and which practices to prioritize for their classroom. Each chapter provides a variety of strategies, allowing teachers the freedom to choose practices that fit their individual situation and comfort level. *Equitable Grading Unlocked* offers teacher-proven strategies that are not only practical but efficient and respectful of the complexities of teaching and learning, workload, and the time limitations all teachers face.

—**Cathy Vatterott**
Professor Emeritus of Education, University of Missouri—St. Louis
Author of *Rethinking Grading*

This book is outstanding. I was up late cheering as I read it. Howard Yank and Maika Yeigh have assembled as comprehensive an analysis of keys to effective formative assessment and grading practices as I have seen. They attend to the emotional dynamics of being evaluated from the student's point of view and of separating formative from summative feedback in ways that maximize student academic confidence and learning success. Their recommended assessment practices are backed by three decades of rigorous international research linking them to profound gains in student academic confidence, engagement, and achievement.

—Rick Stiggins
Founder of Assessment Training Institute
Author of *Give Our Students the Gift of Confidence*

For teachers looking for a thoughtful and practical companion on the journey to implement grading practices to support growth in learning and achievement for all students, I recommend *Equitable Grading Unlocked*. By examining common equitable grading themes, the authors introduce us to scores of teachers and allow us to learn how they approached the many challenges to make the shift to better support student learning.

—Ken Kunin
Head of School, International School Nido de Aguilas, Santiago, Chile

Equitable Grading Unlocked is a bold, practical guide that empowers educators to replace inequitable grading with strategies that honor student voice, foster authentic learning, and advance educational justice. Howard Yank and Maika Yeigh offer a timely, necessary resource for educators committed to justice. As an equity-centered practitioner, I value how the authors blend research, teacher voice, and practical strategies to dismantle biased grading systems. This book doesn't offer quick fixes; rather, it provides adaptable tools, honest stories, and a road map for courageous change. It equips educators to move beyond compliance and build grading practices that honor authentic learning and every student's potential.

—Andratesha Fritzgerald
CEO, Building Blocks of Brilliance
Author of *Antiracism and Universal Design for Learning*

Equitable Grading Unlocked is a remarkable resource for teachers, teacher educators, curriculum developers, and test developers. Its solid grounding in research combined with its strong conceptual frameworks and insightful examples create a symphony of ideas and methods that apply to a wide variety of classroom settings. Clearly and cogently written, Howard Yank and Maika Yeigh give readers what they need to reframe their thinking and practices in ways that will engage students more deeply, enabling them to take greater ownership of their learning.

—**David T. Conley**
Professor emeritus of educational policy and leadership,
University of Oregon
Author of *The Promise and Practice of Next Generation Assessment*

Filled with relevant information from both researchers and classroom teachers, *Equitable Grading Unlocked* describes concrete steps educators can take to enhance their assessment process. There are so many clear examples and relevant suggestions for shifting current grading practices, from actual templates to reflection prompts and practical strategies. This text really bridges the gap for educators who want their grading to be equitable but lack the tools to do so.

—**Elizabeth Denevi**
Director, Eastern Educational Resource Collaborative
Cohost of *Teaching While White* podcast
Author of *Integrating Educator Well-Being, Growth, and Evaluation*

Equitable Grading Unlocked

Equitable Grading Unlocked

PRACTICAL STRATEGIES FROM THE CLASSROOM

HOWARD YANK | MAIKA YEIGH

Arlington, Virginia USA

2111 Wilson Boulevard, Suite 300 • Arlington, VA 22201 USA
Phone: 800-933-2723 or 703-578-9600
Website: www.ascd.org • Email: member@ascd.org
Author guidelines: www.ascd.org/write

Richard Culatta, *Chief Executive Director;* Genny Ostertag, *Managing Director, Book Acquisitions and Editing;* Susan Hills, *Senior Acquisitions Editor;* Mary Beth Nielsen, *Director, Book Editing;* Jamie Greene, *Senior Editor;* Jennifer Morgan, *Editor;* Georgia Park, *Graphic Designer;* Circle Graphics, *Typesetter;* Kelly Marshall, *Production Manager;* Christopher Logan, *Senior Production Specialist;* Shajuan Martin, *E-Publishing Specialist*

Copyright © 2026 ASCD. All rights reserved. It is illegal to reproduce copies of this work, in whole or part, in print or electronic format (including reproductions displayed on a secure intranet or stored in a retrieval system or other electronic storage device from which copies can be made or displayed) without the prior written permission of the publisher. Furthermore, no part of this work may be used or reproduced in any manner for the purpose of training artificial intelligence technologies or systems or development of machine learning language models. The author and publisher expressly reserve all rights to license uses of this work for generative AI training and development of machine learning language models. For permission to reproduce, display, or republish excerpts of this work in print or electronic format, please contact Copyright Clearance Center (CCC), 222 Rosewood Dr., Danvers, MA 01923, USA (www.copyright.com). Send translation inquiries to translations@ascd.org. For any other reuse, submit requests to permissions@ascd.org. Address all other inquiries to books@ascd.org.

ASCD® is a registered trademark of Robin Merger Corporation, Inc. All other trademarks contained in this book are the property of, and reserved by, their respective owners, and are used for editorial and informational purposes only. No such use should be construed to imply sponsorship or endorsement of the book by the respective owners.

All links in this book are correct as of the publication date below but may have become inactive or otherwise modified since that time. If you notice a broken link, please email books@ascd.org; include "Link Update" in the subject line; and in the message, specify the link, the book title, and the page number on which the link appears.

PAPERBACK ISBN: 978-1-4166-3405-8   ASCD product #126009   n1/26
PDF EBOOK ISBN: 978-1-4166-3406-5; see Books in Print for other formats.

Quantity discounts are available: email programteam@ascd.org or call 800-933-2723, ext. 5773, or 703-575-5773. For desk copies, go to www.ascd.org/deskcopy.

Library of Congress Cataloging-in-Publication Data is available for this title.

Library of Congress Control Number: 2025039102

32 31 30 29 28 27 26   1 2 3 4 5 6 7 8 9 10 11 12

To my wife, Karrie Yank—for her patience with the "Office Closed" sign on the door, her unwavering support through the endless hours I disappeared into this project, and her constant encouragement and keen insight that helped carry the work forward. To our dog, Barkley, who lay faithfully at my feet, always ready for a trip to the park when I needed a break. And to my coauthor, Maika—eleven years ago, you sparked a professional partnership that has grown into something truly impactful. It has enriched my practice and, more importantly, touched the practices and lives of countless teachers along the way.

—Howard

To Team Yeigh: The three of you are my foundation and pit crew. Ted, you are always the first to offer encouragement and support for whatever I attempt—including this book. You ask hard questions, problem-solve tricky situations, and encourage me to keep going and reach my goals. Will and Ella, I am so grateful that you both were willing to be my sounding board throughout this project, including providing me with counterpoints, the student point of view, and pushing me forward on my equity journey. I rely on my pit crew often and you always prop me back up and send me back out. Thank you.

To my teacher candidates—past, current, and future—thank you for your willingness to problematize assessment practices in your classrooms and explore more equitable ways together; each year I learn more, and for that I am grateful.

And to my coauthor Howard—in 2014, we developed our first assessment course. Who would have thought we would end up writing a book?

—Maika

Equitable Grading Unlocked

Acknowledgments xiii

Introduction 1

1. Practice Work: *Uncoupling Practice from Grading* 7

2. Grades Versus Feedback: *How to Prevent One from Getting in the Way of the Other* 27

3. Rubrics and Progress Tracking: *Breaking Down Barriers to Grade Transparency* 51

4. Redos and Retakes Done Right: *Avoiding Miscues and Missteps* 83

5. Untimely and Unfinished: *Alternatives to Punitive Late-Work Policies* 99

6. Upgrading Your Gradebook: *Transitioning to Practices That Reflect Student Learning* 115

7. Schoolwide Implementation of New Grading Practices: *Creating Consistency Across Classrooms* 136

References 149

Index 156

About the Authors 161

Study Guide 164

Acknowledgments

Sustainable school change is complex—especially when it challenges long-standing practices like grading. Although many recognize that traditional grading systems are inequitable, moving from awareness to meaningful implementation is a far more difficult journey.

This book exists because of the educators who have taken that journey. They've wrestled with hard questions, navigated pushback, and worked tirelessly to build systems that better reflect student learning and honor diverse strengths. Their skills as teachers have been honed along the way. These teachers remind us that changing grading practices isn't just a technical task—it's emotional and relational work rooted in deep commitment to equity.

We are deeply grateful to the practitioners whose expertise, reflections, and lived experiences have shaped this book. Their methods and voices are not simply referenced—they are centered. Their willingness to experiment, reflect, and lead has moved this work forward in powerful ways. To the following educators: thank you.

Brennan Brockbank, science coordinator, physics teacher	David Douglas School District, Portland, OR
Jake Carlsen, English teacher	Newport High School, Newport, OR
Joel Compton, social studies teacher	Acalanes High School, Orinda, CA
Sara Daley, former mathematics teacher	Portland, OR

Osvaldo Díaz, Spanish teacher	Santa Cruz High School, Santa Cruz, CA
Alex Doucette, social studies teacher	White Bear Lake High School, White Bear Lake, MN
LaRee Ghassemi, mathematics teacher	Rose Hill Middle School, Redmond, WA
Adam Green, science and mathematics teacher	Stockdale High School, Bakersfield, CA
Katie Green, English teacher	Highland High School, Bakersfield, CA
Kim Haber, science teacher	Rose Hill Middle School, Redmond, WA
Katherine Holden, director	The Siskiyou School, Ashland, OR
Michelle Hubbard, French teacher	Santa Cruz High School, Santa Cruz, CA
Eric Jensen, visual arts teacher	David Douglas High School, Portland, OR
Breanne Johnson, social studies teacher	Boring Middle School, Boring, OR
Tim King, social studies teacher	Sherwood High School, Sherwood, OR
Timothy Larsen, science teacher	Vancouver iTech Preparatory, Vancouver, WA
Katie Linklater, science teacher	Rose Hill Middle School, Redmond, WA
Emily Longnecker, social studies teacher	Thomas S. Hart Middle School, Pleasanton, CA
Sergio López, Spanish teacher	New Haven, CT
Laura Mundorff, English teacher	Rex Putnam High School, Milwaukie, OR
Conor O'Brien, social studies teacher	Santa Cruz High School, Santa Cruz, CA
John Reafleng, Spanish teacher	Terra Nova High School, Pacifica, CA
Daniel Robinette, physics teacher (retired)	Clackamas High School, Clackamas, OR

Collin Stegner, band teacher	Judson Middle School, Salem, OR
Dylan Thelan, English teacher	Academy of Arts, Careers, and Technology, Reno, NV
Kristen Tollefsen, associate principal	Rose Hill Middle School, Redmond, WA
Rachel Veto, modern languages department head	Beaver Country Day School, Chestnut Hill, MA
Jennifer Woo, Spanish teacher	Wilcox High School, Santa Clara, CA
Isaiah Wyckoff, visual arts teacher	Vancouver iTech Preparatory, Vancouver, WA
Shuang Yang, Chinese teacher	Harvard-Westlake School, Los Angeles, CA

Howard Yank
Camas, Washington

Maika Yeigh
Portland, Oregon

Introduction

Picture this: You settle into your usual spot in the faculty lounge with your colleague Rose. Today, instead of your typical casual conversation, Rose launches into a frustrated account of her recent attempts to implement more equitable grading practices.

"I thought I was doing the right thing," she sighs, her brow furrowed. "I told my students they'd be fine as long as they met the standards by the end of the term. But it backfired spectacularly! Half the class simply stopped doing any work at all." She shakes her head, continuing, "And don't get me started on the retake opportunities. I gave up countless lunches to offer these options, but hardly anyone showed up. The few who did weren't even the students who needed it most. What am I doing wrong?"

As you listen, you feel a mix of compassion for Rose's frustration and recognition that there's more to the situation than meets the eye. You consider the complexities of changing grading practices and the challenges of student motivation. And you wonder to yourself, *Honestly, how many students would willingly give up their lunch period for a test, regardless of the circumstances?*

You realize this moment is an opportunity for a deeper discussion about effective implementation of equitable grading practices, student engagement, and the nuances of educational reform. But where do you even start?

An Uncomfortable Status Quo

Many traditional grading practices persist in the U.S. education system due more to inertia than to pedagogical merit. The 100-point scale, grading on a curve, and rigid deadlines exemplify entrenched practices that warrant reevaluation or abandonment.

Recent cognitive research has illuminated the ways conventional grading practices can significantly demotivate and deflate adolescent learners (Gkintoni et al., 2023; Macrine & Fugate, 2021; Wilcox et al., 2021), highlighting the need for change in our assessment methods. For example, Feldman (2020) reports that penalizing late submissions and grading formative work inadvertently increases student anxiety and stress. Conventional grading systems also exacerbate inequities for traditionally underserved populations—students of color, those with learning disabilities or challenges, and multilingual learners—by embedding systemic biases and conflating academic mastery with behavioral compliance (Downey & Pribesh, 2004). Additionally, the 100-point scale skews toward failure, making it nearly impossible for students facing early setbacks to recover, and weighted categories often prioritize arbitrary metrics like homework completion, favoring students with greater access to resources and support systems.

And it's not just students who suffer. For many teachers, grading can feel like the hardest and most stressful part of the job (Tierney, 2013). This conflict between valuing student growth and perpetuating timeworn practices has driven teachers to seek more equitable grading methods.

Reimagining our assessment systems offers an opportunity to foster motivation, cultivate a positive learning mindset, and build cultural responsiveness (Hammond, 2015). Grading reform is crucial not only to equitably supporting all populations of students but also to ensuring that our grading practices accurately reflect student learning. Traditional grading often fails to capture the true extent of a student's knowledge and skills, raising questions about its validity as an assessment tool. By critically examining and reforming grading practices, teachers can create a more equitable, motivating, and accurate system of student evaluation that aligns with current understandings of cognitive development and educational psychology.

New Professional Mindset

Teachers' journeys toward changing their grading practices can stem from any number of diverse sources of inspiration and reflection. Shifting perspectives might arise due to collegial discussions, personal observations of student struggles, or a growing awareness of inequities within the education system. LaRee Ghassemi, a middle school math teacher, observes that teachers are sometimes married to the status quo, committed to "the old philosophies because they think it is fair" rather than asking themselves, *Is this the right thing to do?* She credits another teacher for sparking her interest in equitable grading by getting her to reflect on her grading practices: "She challenged me on some things, and I started thinking that she had some good points."

For others, the impetus for change comes from witnessing student disengagement under traditional grading methods. Collin Stegner, a middle school band teacher, felt he "had to make the learning accessible. . . . It wasn't like I was making things easier for them, but 'holding them accountable' made them shut down. And if they shut down, then they were not doing anything." A discussion with his principal caused Spanish teacher John Reafleng to reflect on the idea that "a student's grade should not be determined by what teacher you have," highlighting the importance of consistency and learning-focused grading as core principles of equitable assessment.

Meeting the Challenges of Grading Reform

There is a growing recognition among educators that traditional grading practices often fall short in promoting equity, engagement, and accurate assessment of student learning. The teachers quoted here are only a small part of the expanding conversation about the need for more equitable and effective assessment strategies in education. Despite this increasing recognition of the need for grading reform, implementation remains challenging. Educators face multiple obstacles, including entrenched systems, technological limitations, resistance from stakeholders accustomed to traditional methods, and the complex task of shifting deeply rooted cultural norms related to grading.

These kinds of challenges can leave teachers feeling isolated, whether they are just beginning to consider change or already well on their way to implementing equitable practices. A solitary journey can be daunting, with colleagues sometimes resisting anything that might disrupt established classroom norms. Kristen Tollefsen, an associate middle school principal, shares, "Grading reforms were on my mind, but it felt taboo to discuss them—as if it was everyone's private domain. Yet I longed for these conversations because I knew my approach was flawed. I was giving arbitrary percentages—50 percent for this, 20 percent for that—and I couldn't help but question the rationale. . . . I began experimenting on my own; it was intuitive, but I was navigating uncharted waters alone."

Changing the Conversation

Transforming long-standing teaching practices calls for intentional reflection and implementation. What were once private discussions among educators about grading methods are now entering the public sphere, specifically regarding several key issues: (1) the inequity of outdated grading systems, (2) how these systems discourage risk taking and learning, (3) the inaccuracy of these practices in assessing education standards, and (4) the impact of unconscious bias.

This increased awareness has sparked critical conversations and a push for change—accompanied by a shift in focus from mere academic assessment to fostering essential life skills. As physics teacher Dan Robinette describes it, "We're not just training workers; we're trying to teach students how to persist." This perspective underscores the importance of developing grading practices that align with the broader goals of education, promoting persistence, critical thinking, and lifelong learning. The challenge now lies in translating this awareness into actionable changes in grading systems, ensuring they support equitable, accurate, and meaningful assessment of student learning and growth.

The Devil Is in the Details

Many educators struggle with the process of putting more equitable grading into practice. Despite understanding that traditional methods can hinder student learning, teachers often lack clear guidance on how to effectively institute reforms. This gap between theory and best practice can lead to frustration with and abandonment of grading reform initiatives (Guskey, 2021).

Teachers embarking on grading reform often face a series of common hurdles. For example, they may find that simply allowing assessment retakes doesn't automatically lead to improved student performance, leaving them puzzled about how to foster genuine learning gains. Creating effective rubrics, which are crucial for assessment transparency, can be unexpectedly time-consuming. Ungraded homework policies invite concerns about potentially plummeting completion rates and the question of how to maintain student engagement without traditional grading incentives. These challenges both highlight the complexity of implementing equitable grading practices and underscore the need for practical, experience-based guidance.

A Practical Guide to Equitable Grading

This book addresses that critical need. Though many resources provide the rationale for an overhaul of assessment practices, few offer the day-to-day strategies necessary for success. Our focus is on anticipating and overcoming common challenges, providing workable options for grading reform, promoting student ownership of learning, and engaging stakeholders in the process.

Throughout this book, we emphasize the importance of navigating challenges and avoiding pitfalls in the journey toward grading reform—and we explain why the changes are needed at every step. This approach ensures that the book serves a wide audience, from educators just beginning to consider these questions to those who have already made significant progress in rethinking their practices. By providing a comprehensive exploration of both the how and the why of grading reform, this book is a valuable resource for teachers at all stages of this transformative process.

Learning from Experience

The heart of the book lies in the voices of real teachers who have navigated the complexities of grading reform. Many teachers have transformed their classrooms from environments where students chase points to spaces where students learn to take ownership of their learning. This book is about these teachers and their stories, and it's about how they are using grading as a tool for student growth. Their firsthand experiences give invaluable insights into what works in various school contexts. They have essentially beta-tested their equitable grading methods with their students, both individually and collaboratively, to establish, iterate, and refine them. By sharing their strategies, we aim to bridge the gap between theory and successful implementation, empowering educators to construct their own road maps toward grading system reform, ensuring that the initial spark of reform develops into a sustainable and impactful change in educational practice.

Think back to learning to drive, to swing a tennis racket, or to play a musical instrument. Each milestone—a smooth stop, a centered hit, a perfectly tuned string—felt impossibly difficult at first, taking time, practice, and persistence to achieve. Implementing equitable grading practices is similarly complex and demands a similar commitment to learning and growth. We hope the experiences and insights shared in this book will serve as your guide, supporting you as you navigate these challenges and create a more just and effective learning environment for every student.

1

Practice Work

Uncoupling Practice from Grading

Have you ever found yourself overwhelmed by a mountain of student work that has accumulated on your desk or amassed in files on Google Classroom or Canvas? Not only are you daunted by the prospect of grading and recording all this work, but you haven't even started to plan tomorrow's lessons? If so, you are not alone.

The practice of grading student work has long been a cornerstone of education. However, as understanding of effective pedagogy evolves, so too does our approach to assessment. This chapter delves into the contentious issue of grading formative or practice work, challenging the traditional notion that all student efforts must be quantified and recorded. First, we will look at why grading practice work and class participation (despite its prevalence) may be harmful and counterproductive to the goal of education: fostering learning and growth. Then we will focus on the challenges facing teachers who want to move away from scoring everything students produce, presenting options for meeting these challenges and helping students and their families see the connection between practice work and assessment results.

The Pitfalls of Grading Practice Work

In 1986, Butler and Nisan demonstrated that grades can undermine intrinsic motivation and creativity in learning tasks. Grading practice work may seem to hold students accountable, but it can inadvertently create several situations that undermine the learning process. Let's delve into some of these.

Student Stress

One of the most deleterious effects of grading practice work is the stress it places on students. When every assignment carries the weight of a grade, students may find themselves in a constant state of anxiety, fearing that each misstep will negatively affect their academic standing. The perception that the stakes are high creates a high-pressure environment in which students may become overly focused on achieving perfect scores rather than engaging deeply with the material to develop their skills and knowledge. Grading every assignment tends to reduce students' interest in what they are learning and discourages intellectual risk taking (Guskey, 2022; Kohn, 2011). Academic anxiety not only hinders students' ability to learn but also affects their overall well-being and can lead to mental health issues (Leslie, 2021).

Integrity

An emphasis on grading practice work also creates an environment ripe for unethical choices. When students feel that their worth is measured by every grade, including grades on formative assessments, they may resort to dishonest practices to maintain their academic standing. Traditional points-based grading practices can significantly influence the likelihood of academic dishonesty from students who feel they cannot complete practice tasks successfully (Talbert, 2023). When students believe they cannot take risks and make mistakes, it not only undermines the integrity of the educational process but also robs them of valuable learning opportunities.

Teacher Priorities

Grading every piece of practice work creates an enormous burden. Teachers find themselves drowning in a sea of papers to score or grade, leaving little time for activities such as providing meaningful feedback or planning engaging lessons. In their study on grading, Schinske and Tanner (2014) conclude that "the time and stress associated with grading has the potential to distract instructors from other, more meaningful aspects of teaching and learning" (p. 159). Grading every assignment creates a huge downside for both teachers and students, while also limiting the actual benefits of practice work.

The Pitfalls of Grading Class Participation

Some teachers try to encourage student engagement by grading class participation, but this practice has the potential to introduce significant bias and create unintended negative consequences. Grading participation can disproportionately disadvantage introverted students, who may need more time to process information before speaking (Cain, 2012). As noted by Feldman (2024b), this approach can also unfairly affect students with disabilities (e.g., anxiety disorders, speech impediments, processing differences); students from historically marginalized groups who may have different cultural norms around verbal participation; and multilingual learners, who may be less confident in their English skills.

Moreover, the pressure to participate for a grade can inhibit students' oral processing and thoughtful contributions. Students may feel compelled to speak up even when they haven't fully formulated their ideas, leading to superficial comments rather than meaningful discourse (Brookhart, 2013). And as Hattie and Timperley (2007) note, anxiety can significantly interfere with a student's ability to process and respond to classroom discussions. Finally, grading oral participation does not account for less visible but valuable forms of engagement such as active listening or written reflections (Zwiers & Crawford, 2011).

One of the most insidious effects of grading class participation is that it is a form of extrinsic motivation. When students become accustomed to receiving grades for every task, their motivation shifts from a genuine desire to learn to a pursuit of external rewards. This focus on extrinsic rewards can lead to a shallow approach to learning, in which students prioritize short-term grade acquisition over deep understanding and long-term retention of knowledge. As Anderson (2019) stresses in his book on the connection between teacher language and student learning, "We don't want the tail of student desire to get a good grade to wag the dog of student learning" (pp. 112–113).

Science teacher Kim Haber, who has been transitioning away from grading every student assignment for five years, emphasizes the importance of authentic engagement over point tracking. She notes that the change hasn't resulted in any lessening of student participation in her classroom. "Students want to feel successful. If you're setting up really engaging ways to learn, students will want to participate—you don't have to track it. And then you can spend your energy on the students who are not engaging [with the lesson] and find out what is going on with them."

Maintaining Student Engagement and Motivation

The power of practice is thoroughly acknowledged in sports and competitive pursuits, yet we often overlook its importance in academic settings. Accomplished coaches or music conductors are unlikely to threaten point deductions to inspire their teams or ensembles, instead relying on the motivation of the desire to perform well on game or concert day. Although Malcolm Gladwell's 10,000-hour rule may be an oversimplification of how to develop expertise (Gladwell, 2008), it underscores the crucial role of dedicated practice in high achievement.

The fear of losing the perceived safety net of traditional grading can be paralyzing. Educators who have moved away from grading practice work have discovered a surprising truth, however: Student productivity does not decline. In fact, many report increased engagement and a transformation of their teaching practice. Katherine Holden, who was a teacher and then associate principal at a middle school in Oregon that has endeavored to separate grades from practice work, shares that the school's results were surprising:

> Some teachers really believed kids were not going to turn in assignments in the new system, but we did a data analysis a couple of years ago looking at how many missing assignments there were currently compared with our former traditional gradebook system at the same time of year. The number had decreased by more than half.

Cultivating Classroom Culture and Routines

In a classroom environment that nurtures social and emotional learning, students feel safe to take risks and learn from mistakes. Teachers can foster collaboration through peer-to-peer processing, team problem solving and analysis related to the subject, and class discussions about essential questions or effective strategies. When students perceive that their teachers are passionate about what they teach and genuinely care about student learning, intrinsic motivation flourishes. As John Reafleng, a high school Spanish teacher, notes,

> When it comes to motivating students to be involved in participating in practice work, you really have to set the culture early on in the school

year, where "this is just what we do." So, from the start, I don't grade practice. I stopped using participation as criteria for grades. Most kids say, "OK, I get it. It's practice." Others say, "How much is this worth in the gradebook?" But those questions diminish over time.

Foregrounding the learning process over grades helps address inequities in education and fosters an inclusive learning environment that recognizes that students come from diverse backgrounds and may have different starting points in their educational journey. By reframing practice work as an integral part of the learning process rather than a graded obligation, teachers can reignite students' natural curiosity and desire for improvement. Focusing on growth and improvement rather than just final outcomes creates a more equitable system that values each student's individual progress.

Cultivating Learning: Process over Grades

Shifting the focus from grades to the learning process relies on two key strategies: emphasizing the value of practice and incorporating reflection. Continual discussion of how practice leads to improvement helps students develop a growth mindset, teaching them that abilities develop through effort and strategies. Sharing stories of perseverance, especially ones relevant to students from disadvantaged backgrounds, demonstrates that challenges can be overcome. Providing detailed feedback on students' growth and skill development reinforces the value of practice and connects it to real-world outcomes.

Teaching reflective practices and incorporating them into lessons allows students to take ownership of their learning. When students set learning goals (e.g., "I want to understand photosynthesis"), it helps them articulate their aspirations and track their progress. Reflection enhances their understanding of individual learning processes and connects learning to personal experiences, making education more accessible. Reflection can take the form of learning journals, student portfolios, or exit tickets—even ones as simple as "What was the most surprising thing you learned today?"—to reinforce learning and connection to prior knowledge.

Such approaches to practice work empower students and can especially benefit those from marginalized groups. And engaging in reflective practices yourself can better equip you to address biases and adapt your teaching to meet diverse learner needs.

Making Practice Meaningful and Relevant

Connecting practice activities to real-world applications or student interests is crucial to engagement. In a physics class, for example, problems can be framed around designing roller coasters or optimizing sports equipment to make abstract concepts more tangible and interesting for students. Tying practice to real-life situations helps students see the value of their learning. This can increase engagement and motivation, particularly for students who may feel disconnected from traditional academic content.

Explaining the purpose behind a practice assignment also helps students understand its value. In a literature class, the teacher might explain how analyzing poetry enhances critical thinking skills applicable in many areas of life. Taking this concept further, meaningful practice that addresses real-world problems helps students learn to identify and challenge societal inequities. For example, many teachers use the writings of Langston Hughes and Maya Angelou to show how art can confront racial and economic disparities.

Allowing student choice in practice activities, when possible, caters to diverse interests and can enhance engagement. Offering options helps students take ownership of their learning, fostering independence and decision-making skills. In a social studies class, for example, students might choose between creating a podcast, writing an essay, or designing a mind map to demonstrate their understanding of a historical event.

By implementing practices like these, educators can create a more equitable learning environment that values individual growth, encourages reflection, and makes learning relevant to all students, regardless of their background or initial skill level. Moving away from a one-size-fits-all model of education toward a more inclusive, culturally responsive approach can help address systemic inequities in education, leveling the playing field and giving every student the opportunity to recognize and celebrate their own progress and achievements.

These kinds of strategies are especially crucial in secondary schools, where student inquisitiveness tends to wane as the emphasis on scores and grades becomes more prominent. As noted by Engel in *The Hungry Mind: The Origins of Curiosity in Childhood* (2015), the increasing focus on standardized testing and grade-based assessments in higher grades often comes at the expense of students' innate drive to explore and question. Relieving practice from the pressure of grades creates an environment that nurtures an intrinsic motivation to learn, encouraging students to engage with material out of genuine interest rather than for external rewards. This shift away from a transactional classroom can help counteract the trend of diminishing curiosity and foster a more authentic and enduring love of learning.

Collaborative Learning

A more organically felt benefit can be enjoyed by students every day from the process of learning together with their peers. Dewey's theories of learning (1916, 1938) emphasize interactions and communications focused on enhancing shared meanings. Viewing knowledge as socially constructed, he advocated for cooperative and collaborative learning environments.

Science teacher Kim Haber puts Dewey's principles into practice by having her 6th graders work collaboratively to develop their conceptual understanding. Students regularly organize into small groups to analyze scientific models, fostering active discussion and collective problem solving. Student teams engage in thorough dialogue, reaching a consensus before documenting their response to questions posed.

Kim plays an active role in this process, reviewing each group's work at designated checkpoints that prevent them from advancing before they have a solid grasp on the current concepts. To ensure individual accountability and prevent passive participation, she randomly selects team members to explain their group's reasoning. This encourages all students to engage fully with the material and be prepared to articulate their understanding. During these check-ins, Kim often poses probing questions designed to address any misconceptions she observes or to challenge students to think more deeply about the concepts at hand.

Strengthening Students' Skills

The iterative process of group work, instructor review, and further discussion creates a dynamic learning environment that promotes deep understanding and critical thinking. Kim Haber credits the process with keeping students engaged and accountable without the pressure of grades. To support students in working together, which may be a developing skill, it is important to establish team norms and team roles, such as facilitator, timekeeper, and reporter. Teachers can provide as added support a visual aid that defines or describes the different roles and responsibilities.

Protocols to Support Understanding

Collaborative skills are not intuitive. Without scaffolds, student teams may become dysfunctional, with one or two kids doing all the work and others left to their own devices. This less-than-ideal outcome may lead teachers to abandon group work entirely, which in turn results in students feeling more isolated and losing the motivation that is intrinsic in the collaborative process.

Using structured protocols for teamwork offers significant benefits for a diverse range of students and helps create a more equitable and culturally responsive learning environment. Robust, structured talk formats encourage participation from students who might otherwise remain silent or passive (Hammond, 2020). This includes multilingual learners, shy students, disengaged learners, and those from historically marginalized backgrounds.

Incorporating such frameworks into lessons creates opportunities for what Hammond (2014) calls "cognitive chewing," allowing students to process information and formulate ideas in ways that align with their cultural backgrounds and learning styles. These frameworks honor the diverse knowledge base each student brings to the conversation, giving marginalized students greater access to the flow of discussion and more agency in directing it. Protocols are particularly effective in breaking the pattern of having the same students—typically those who are comfortable with English, possess mainstream background knowledge, or are more extroverted—dominate class discussions. Instead, protocols create entry points for a wider range of voices, making the learning experience more inclusive. By centering these practices around principles of youth culture and collectivist practice, teachers can further enhance the cultural responsiveness of the classroom, ensuring that all students feel valued and empowered to contribute to the learning process.

Priorities to Pique Student Engagement

When grades are no longer the main source of motivation, teachers must cultivate students' natural curiosity, encouraging genuine interest in their learning and deeper, more meaningful engagement with both their work and their peers. Collaboration and communication should be seamlessly integrated into daily academic activities, with assessments focused on students' ability to understand and apply essential concepts related to course content. It is equally important to cultivate habits of mind such as intellectual openness and communication skills, which are crucial for effective teamwork and bolster social and emotional learning. These habits of mind are skills that will position students in good stead for success in college and beyond (Conley, 2010). By prioritizing these competencies, even without scoring or grading students' performance of them, teachers prepare students not only for academic success but also for lifelong learning and adaptability in their personal and professional lives.

Cultivating a learning culture that is not tied to daily scores or grades represents a significant shift in pedagogical practice. Weaning students from a dependency on graded practice work is most effectively achieved through a phased approach. By implementing changes gradually, you can identify and address potential challenges or resistance early on, ensuring a smoother transition and greater acceptance over time. We suggest the following steps:

1. **Introduce the concept and set expectations.** Explain to students the value of practice in the learning process, discuss how disconnecting practice work from grades will benefit their long-term learning and skill development, and set clear expectations for participation and engagement in practice activities.
2. **Start with low-stakes practice activities.** Incorporate ungraded practice work into class activities, provide feedback focused on improvement (rather than score), and use ungraded formative assessments to gauge understanding.
3. **Reduce emphasis on grades for practice work.** First reduce the weight of practice work grades within the overall grade, then shift toward a completion-based system for practice work (rather than accuracy-based grading). Eventually, eliminate grading for all designated practice activities.
4. **Refine regular routines around practice.** Schedule daily or weekly dedicated practice time with rituals for starting and ending practice, and consistently reinforce the importance of practice in the learning process.
5. **Align assessments with practice focus.** Ensure that formal assessments reflect the skills practiced, allow students to use their practice work to prepare for assessments, and provide opportunities for students to revise work based on practice and feedback.

Providing dedicated practice time and aligning assessments with practice ensures that all students have equal opportunities to develop skills and prepare for assessments within the school environment. This can help mitigate disparities caused by differences in home environments or access to tutoring. Overall, this promotes a more equitable learning environment by valuing effort, growth, and mastery over initial performance or external advantages.

Measured implementation benefits teachers as well, especially those who prefer to proceed cautiously with new methods. Kim Haber recommends that teachers who might be hesitant to embark on a dramatic shift take it slow: "If you are skeptical about students losing motivation because you're not grading everything or you're not incentivizing with a grade, give it a try. Take one small piece at a time." Phasing in or scaffolding new ways of working aligns with established principles of effective pedagogy. This approach allows for adjustment, reflection, and refinement at each stage, ultimately leading to more successful and sustainable changes in grading practices.

Katie Linklater, a science teacher at the same school as Kim, starts the uncoupling process with her students' science notebook.

> They ask, "Is this graded?" I'll say, "Well, that's part of your notebook grade." I do grade the first notebook check, so they see the value in it. Then, later in the year, we get to the point where I can say, "Your notebook is something that can help you and is a place where you practice." I talk about why it's important to do the assignment. It gets kids to want to engage.

Although Katie has moved away from scoring student notebooks entirely, other teachers continue to give students at least some credit for this kind of formative work. Science teacher Rob Ickes (2024) doesn't grade notebooks but allows students to use their "field notes" during tests, explaining, "This approach has decreased my students' anxiety and given them more incentive to 'practice harder,' knowing their practice will yield better results in their 'big game'" (para. 8).

The transition to a classroom culture of ungraded practice can be implemented through a phased, gradually progressing process that addresses the interplay of the variety of factors involved. Deeply ingrained expectations about grading held by students, teachers, parents, and administrators create resistance to change. Students need time to adapt and develop intrinsic motivation, and teachers must learn how to adjust their assessment strategies and teaching methods. Misconceptions about ungraded systems require ongoing education, and stakeholders often want to see evidence of effectiveness before fully embracing the change. Ultimately, the transition demands patience, persistence, and continuous efforts to shift not only practices but also deeply rooted mindsets and cultural norms.

Spotlight: Practice Work
Laura Mundorff, English Language Arts
Putnam High School, Milwaukie, Oregon

Over the years, Laura has learned that students in her English classes need to engage with lots of ungraded, low-stakes practice work to succeed. The students keep a structured composition book, she says, and "most days we work in that journal. I'm very clear about my expectations." One example of a practice assignment is the Prompt of the Day, in which students write responses to a poem, picture, or other prompt. The class knows the routine. "They're expected to fill the entire page if they can. It's informal. It's low-stakes writing. The idea is to get them to build their writing fluency." Laura's students have the opportunity to practice skills, try out ideas, and see how practice helps them with their learning. Students who routinely complete such exercises are more prepared for later summative assessments. Laura notes,

> The formative work that they do in their journals is to prepare them for the assessment. For example, the natural consequence of not doing the dialectical journal is that when it comes to writing the essay, the student won't have any evidence that they can use. Pretty much everything that goes into their journal is something that they're going to need to be successful on the assessment.

In Laura's class, this work is ultimately graded; a complete notebook is worth 30 percent of the overall course grade. However, the primary purpose is for students to take ownership of their own learning through self-assessment.

At the conclusion of each unit, students reflect on their work, set goals for themselves, and self-assess. They first review all assignments from the unit, categorizing each as "exceeds expectations," "meets expectations," "incomplete," or "missing"; this encourages students to critically examine their performance throughout the unit. Next, in response to guided questions intended to prompt deeper reflection, students identify aspects of the unit they found enjoyable, note areas where they experienced growth, and set personal goals for future learning. This reflective process extends beyond academic performance to include class participation and engagement in discussion. As part of this self-evaluation, students assign themselves a score based on an overview of their work throughout the unit. This encourages students to consider their learning experience holistically rather than focusing on individual assignments. Laura reviews these self-evaluation journal entries and uses them to gauge student perceptions and progress.

This comprehensive self-evaluation system provides students with numerous opportunities to develop metacognitive skills, take ownership of their learning, and actively participate in assessment. It not only provides valuable insights for the teacher but also fosters students' ability to critically evaluate their own work and learning strategies. As Laura notes, "It's a very big time-saver for me, and I think it's better for them. I don't think I should be the only audience for all of their writing."

Because Laura spends less time on grading, she can devote her planning period to working with her professional learning community to develop lessons that meet the needs of her students. She also can provide feedback to students during class time. "If I'm not grading the work, they still need to know how they're doing," she explains. Her approach to practice work means "I'm able to spend my time giving feedback in class in person." When she needs to collect more information on student progress or skill attainment, she can either assign a relevant journal prompt or poll the class using a Google Form.

Laura has found that students are willing to complete practice work when they can see how it helps them succeed on the assessment. "It really does give them ownership over their learning in a way that collecting a paper from them every day does not. They have a lot of pride in their work when they walk away with a full notebook. There's a lot of power in them seeing their practice pay off."

Spotlight Questions

- What key insight can you gain from Laura's approach to using practice work?

- Can you identify a task that your students regularly complete that could be more beneficial as ungraded practice work? If you've already implemented ungraded practice, what strategies do you use to encourage students to take greater ownership of their work?
- If you were to stop grading practice work, what valuable activity could you dedicate more time to?
- How do you incorporate self-reflection in your teaching to give students more agency in their learning?
- What specific ideas about ungraded practice work would you like to share or discuss with your colleagues?

Tuning into Practice

Eliminating grades from practice work also helps teachers focus on student needs and progress, whereas grades can sometimes get in the way of improvement. Collin Stegner, a middle school band teacher, focuses on skills practice according to the student needs he sees and hears:

> When kids struggle with making connections, it's often because they're having difficulty with the listening aspect or they simply need more practice and development. If the connection isn't happening, we can do practice exercises the next day or incorporate games and activities focused on improving audiation skills. This approach makes it easy to identify their weaknesses and specifically work on those.

Uncoupling grading from informal assessments and practice work, as Collin does with his students' listening skills, may seem daunting to many educators. However, it's worth noting that this approach has been successfully employed by music teachers for years. This long-standing practice in music education may provide teachers of other subjects with confidence and inspiration to implement similar strategies.

Ungraded Homework

Uncoupling grading from practice work can also be applied to the culture around homework. Rachel Veto, head of a modern languages department, has helped her students approach homework differently. Their homework is optional and not graded; instead, she says, students have options such as "either complete two homework assignments during the week or take a quiz on Friday. Neither affects their grade." Her choice board of assignments is divided into categories of reading, writing, listening, and speaking, which allows for student choice about what practice might benefit them the most and bolsters ownership of their own learning (see Figure 1.1 for a sample from an introductory French conversation class).

FIGURE 1.1
French I Assignment Choice Board

Read the text and answer the questions	Watch a video on edPuzzle	Explain	Create
Charlotte	Introducing the Family	What are your family's preferences?	Instagram post (minimum three sentences with vocabulary)
Tal's Biography	I Introduce Myself	Describe a celebrity	Create a puzzle (word search, crossword, etc., with vocabulary)
Harry Potter	Teenagers' Sports	Explain a famous complicated family	Practice with vocab cards or Quizlet
Email from Senegal	Descriptions	Describe a photo of a group of friends	Write a description of activities you do with your friends
An article on the internet that you understand and can explain	A grammar video from the list	Respond to a classmate	Create a family tree with seven sentences of explanation

The Turning Point

Getting to a point of inflection, when teachers realize that the culture around grades has significantly changed for the better, is a journey with a long arc. Emily Longnecker, a middle school history teacher, has been collaboratively refining assessment practices with her grade-level teams for three years. The progress has been more pronounced with her 8th grade colleagues, a smaller group, compared with the larger 7th grade team. This difference in advancement illustrates one of the challenges mentioned earlier: the time-consuming nature of aligning all stakeholders with new education approaches. Despite the varying rates of adoption among her colleagues, Emily reports that the transition has successfully taken root in her own classroom:

> Students are now focusing on their learning rather than just chasing points. Instead of asking why they got 96 points instead of 97, they're asking what they need to do to improve their understanding. In my class, the emphasis is on what knowledge they need to acquire and what standards they need to meet, not on making up missed work or stressing about grades. This approach allows struggling students to experience success through effort and persistence, which is a significant part of their learning journey. It's a stark contrast to other places, where students are still fixated on points and grades for every assignment.

Engaging Families in the Process

It's not just the students who need time to adapt to a different pedagogical approach; other stakeholders need to be brought on board as well. High school teacher Alex Doucette finds that families respond positively when he keeps communication open, describing the goals of his approach as a continuous cycle of instruction, practice, and feedback. He tells students, "It's like shooting free throws in basketball; it's all about consistent practice." Alex says the open communication "has significantly shifted the culture around grades."

Although Alex has not encountered significant pushback from parents, other teachers may find that families have substantial concerns about academic standards and expectations. Many parents, accustomed to traditional grading systems, may perceive the absence of grades on practice work as a lowering of academic standards or a reduction in rigor. This misperception can lead to resistance and skepticism about the effectiveness of ungraded practice, even as research and experience show that removing grades from practice work can lead to improved performance on summative assessments and a deeper understanding of the material.

Grades are often viewed as a clear indicator of a student's progress and academic standing. The familiarity of letter grades and percentages provides a sense of security and a seemingly objective measure of achievement. When these recognizable markers are removed from practice work, it can create anxiety and uncertainty. How will families know if a student is making progress? Will students be motivated to complete work that isn't graded? Are teachers lowering their expectations by not grading every assignment? How will this practice affect students' college applications or future opportunities?

Grading is "deeply ingrained not only in education but in our culture" (Vatterott, 2015, p. 6) as the primary measure of academic success; it often goes unquestioned by those who experienced similar systems in their own schooling. The community may be accustomed or conditioned to have everything students do count in their grade. Making a shift in grading practices calls into question these assumptions. Therefore, it is incumbent upon educators to communicate how ungraded practice work can lead to higher standards and improved student performance and to allay apprehensions and highlight the benefits of ungraded practice work. Here are a few suggestions:

- **Provide clear explanations.** Clearly communicate the rationale behind ungraded practice work, emphasizing its connection to improved learning outcomes and performance on summative assessments.
- **Offer detailed progress reports.** Provide students and families with regular, detailed feedback on student progress, including areas of strength and opportunities for growth.
- **Demonstrate the link to summative performance.** Communicate how ungraded practice work translates to improved performance on graded, summative assessments. Share research findings that highlight the benefits of ungraded practice work on student learning and achievement along with data from a class in the school or area that has made this transition to underscore its effectiveness.

- **Highlight real-world connections.** Explain how ungraded practice echoes real-world learning and problem solving, where the focus is on improvement and solutions rather than arbitrary scores.

Grade Inflation Versus High Standards

Sharing research with parents and families is crucial to communicating the validity of alternative grading practices and addressing concerns about the issue of grade inflation. Both educators and families want grades to accurately reflect student learning and mastery of content. However, traditional grading practices, particularly the grading of practice work, can lead to inflated grades that do not accurately reflect student performance.

Practice assignments are designed for learning and making mistakes, not demonstrating mastery—yet teachers frequently grade these assignments based on completion or effort rather than understanding. Students may seek help or collaborate on these tasks, which—although beneficial to learning—may result in higher grades that do not represent their independent abilities. The accumulation of high marks on numerous practice assignments can outweigh lower scores on more comprehensive assessments, skewing the overall grade.

Grading practice work can also shift students' focus from deep learning to the shallow pursuit of correct answers, leading to superficial understanding that is not up to more rigorous evaluation. Teachers might also grade practice work more leniently to encourage participation, inadvertently inflating grades without a corresponding increase in actual learning.

Collectively, these factors create a significant disconnect between assigned grades and students' true level of understanding or ability to apply knowledge independently, particularly when compared with performance on standardized tests or real-world applications of skills. This discrepancy becomes especially apparent when comparing course grades to standardized test scores like the ACT and SAT, knowing that both grades and test scores are often crucial for college admissions.

Feldman (2024a) found that nearly 60 percent of grades did not match students' standardized test scores. Approximately two-thirds of these mismatched grades were inflated, while about a third were depressed. This inconsistency not only creates confusion but also leads to unrealistic expectations and potential disappointment when students face standardized assessments or college-level work. Focusing grades on summative assessments rather than practice work reduces inaccuracy and addresses grade inflation while providing a more realistic picture of student achievement.

The transition to ungraded practice work may initially cause concern among families, caregivers, and other stakeholders. It is important to emphasize that this approach leads to higher standards and better academic outcomes. By focusing on the learning process, providing meaningful feedback, and encouraging risk taking and creativity, ungraded practice work prepares students more effectively for summative assessments and real-world challenges. Students and their families need to understand that the absence of grades on practice work does not equate to a lowering of standards. Instead, it represents a shift toward a more effective, equitable, and meaningful approach to learning. By clearly communicating benefits and addressing concerns, we can encourage families to engage with the learning process by reviewing feedback and discussing progress, rather than focusing solely on grades.

Student and Family Feedback

Although most teachers regularly provide feedback to students, they do not often *seek* feedback from parents, caregivers, or the students themselves regarding the changes they implement in the classroom—particularly those related to grading practices. Seeking feedback on grading reforms such as not grading practice work is crucial to ensuring the success and acceptance of these changes. Engaging with these key stakeholders provides several benefits that can enhance the effectiveness of grading reforms and foster a more supportive education environment.

First, feedback from students can offer valuable insights into how grading reforms affect their learning experience. Students are the primary recipients of these changes, and their perspectives can reveal whether a new approach fosters deeper understanding and engagement or causes confusion and anxiety. Conducting student surveys is an effective way to gather this feedback systematically. A survey might include questions to gauge whether students' feelings of stress have decreased with the uncoupling of grades from practice work, whether student motivation has changed with the increased focus on learning, and whether grades based on summative assessments feel more "fair." Teachers can analyze the results and share them with students (e.g., via Google Forms,

SurveySparrow, Typeform), facilitating discussion about effects of the new protocols on practice work, addressing concerns, or adopting suggestions students might have. This transparency promotes student voice and buy-in.

In addition, involving families and caregivers in the feedback process can play a significant role in supporting a student's education. The understanding and acceptance of grading reforms on the part of the people surrounding students is vital for successful implementation. Sharing student feedback with caregivers can provide a clearer picture of how these changes are perceived by those directly affected. This dialogue helps build trust and transparency between educators and families, fostering a collaborative partnership that benefits student learning.

Data-Driven Approaches

Using data to highlight the connection between students' completion rate of practice assignments and their assessment performance can be a valuable tool for engaging stakeholders. This includes regularly analyzing and sharing classwide and schoolwide trends (using anonymized data) to show how students who consistently complete practice work tend to perform better on summative assessments. Teachers can also encourage individual reflection by having students track their completion rates alongside their assessment scores, which helps them visualize correlations over time. Providing specific examples of how practice assignments directly relate to sample assessment problems, prompts, or questions can illustrate the practical benefits of completing these tasks. By fostering this understanding, teachers can motivate students to engage more fully with practice work as a valuable tool for improving overall academic performance, not just busywork.

Pause and Reflect

Take a look at the following prompts and select a couple that are relevant to you based on where you are in separating practice work from grading. Reflect on your own, discuss with colleagues one-on-one, or start a discussion with your team.

- Among the various drawbacks to grading practice work discussed in this chapter, which do you find most convincing as a reason to modify your teaching approach?

- What strategies are you currently employing to encourage genuine student engagement in your classes without relying on external rewards?
- Which of your existing formative assessment practices do you think could benefit from further development or refinement?
- How crucial is it for you and your colleagues to implement grading practice reforms in concert? How could you initiate or continue discussions with your peers about these topics?
- How might you incorporate student feedback and parental involvement in the process of reforming grading practices?

2

Grades Versus Feedback

How to Prevent One from Getting in the Way of the Other

You spent all weekend grading and adding comments to student work, but how do you know your students are reading your feedback after you return their assignments? How can you inspire students to accept your invitation to revise their work?

Although providing feedback to students has been shown in multiple studies to improve student learning, when students focus more on their grade and less on making improvements to their work, its potential remains untapped (Butler, 1988; Hattie & Timperley, 2007). This phenomenon has significant implications for teaching and learning. As Brookhart (2008) observes, "If a paper is returned with both a grade and a comment, many students will pay attention to the grade and ignore the comment" (p. 8).

The Double-Edged Sword: Mixing Grades with Feedback

The tendency for students to prioritize grades can significantly undermine the potential benefits of feedback, causing them to miss out on targeted guidance for improvement. Grades are often perceived as a more immediate, concrete measure of performance, whereas the value of descriptive feedback that takes effort to address may be less apparent. When work is graded, students are more likely to be motivated by performance goals (i.e., achieving a certain grade) than mastery goals associated with learning (Dlaska & Krekeler, 2017). As Butler and Nisan (1986) report, students who receive only comments on their work show more improvement compared with those receiving both grades and comments. Grades can also overshadow or interfere with a student's processing of descriptive feedback (Schinske & Tanner, 2014).

In addition, mixing grades with teacher feedback can exacerbate inequities. Traditional grading practices often incorporate subjective elements influenced by teachers' implicit biases (Feldman, 2019b), which disproportionately affect students from marginalized groups (Cherng, 2017). What's more, the use of points and grades as extrinsic motivators can undermine students' intrinsic motivation for learning, particularly for those who may already feel marginalized in the education system (Ryan & Deci, 2017). Focusing on grades rather than growth and learning can create a classroom environment that discourages risk taking and authentic engagement, especially for students from historically underserved populations (Feldman, 2019b).

Traditional grading practices typically do not enhance academic motivation; instead, the use of grades can increase students' anxiety to the extent that they avoid taking more challenging courses (Chamberlin et al., 2023; Klapp et al., 2024). Anxiety can further detract from students' willingness to engage deeply with feedback and make substantive improvements to their work. Moreover, a focus on grades can create a transactional relationship between students and teachers, potentially eroding trust.

To address these challenges, we need to reconsider how and when we provide grades in relation to feedback. Students who get feedback before receiving a grade improve more than those who get a grade before feedback (Watson, 2023). As middle school teacher Breanne Johnson notes, "When you hand back the work and they see the grade—that's it. They don't even look at the feedback." The effort you expend crafting precise, helpful comments can be undercut just by adding a grade to the work.

What Makes Feedback Effective?

Feedback is a top influencing factor on student learning (Hattie & Timperley, 2007), a crucial component to helping students understand their progress and take control of their learning journey (Stiggins, 2012). Providing regular feedback emphasizes the ongoing nature of learning, and timely, applicable feedback plays a crucial role in supporting student growth. As Duckor and Holmberg (2024) note, "Feedback links the 'not yet' with the 'here's how,' a stance that foregrounds student learning" (p. 46). To be most effective, feedback should meet the following criteria. It should

- Be timely and actionable.
- Connect both to learning targets and to students' needs and success criteria.
- Emphasize correct responses while highlighting progress, strengths, and areas for improvement.
- Build student ownership and self-esteem and enhance dialogue.
- Incorporate self- and peer assessment.

Specific, actionable, timely feedback can support increased motivation, learning, and self-esteem (Woolf, 2020). With this foundation in mind, let's explore strategies to provide high-quality feedback to students while reducing the time spent on grading. We'll also discuss methods to help students make effective use of feedback to enhance their work and showcase their learning. Recognizing that students may require additional support to fully incorporate teacher feedback, we will present specific techniques for assisting all students, including those who have historically been underserved in schools. These strategies help to make feedback more accessible and actionable for all students.

Streamlining Feedback Processes

Many teachers, especially those with large student loads, find providing high-quality feedback a daunting task. The traditional approach of dedicating weekend hours to grading essays or laboratory reports frequently results in an overwhelming workload. Recognizing this challenge, some teachers have evaluated and adjusted their practices by shifting priorities, streamlining grading processes, or eliminating grading of formative work. English teacher Laura Mundorff explains, "I have to be choosier. I don't grade everything, and I don't enter grades on a daily basis—those are huge time-savers."

Streamlining the feedback process helps you manage your workload while continuing to provide meaningful commentary to students. We envision the classroom as a nurturing environment where growth and understanding take center stage, and teachers move beyond mere error correction. This shift is pivotal in addressing inequities in education, as it opens doors for all students—regardless of their background or starting point—to learn from their mistakes and continuously improve. Such an approach fosters a truly inclusive and effective educational experience, empowering students with the confidence to tackle challenging tasks head-on. Moreover, it equips them with the skills and mindset necessary to excel in graded summative evaluations. Ultimately, an efficient, targeted feedback process doesn't just prepare students for assessments; it cultivates lifelong learners who are resilient, self-aware, and ready to face the complexities of the world beyond the classroom.

Practice Work and Homework as Instructional Tools

Dylan Thelan, a novice English teacher, uses formative assessment to inform his teaching. Instead of assigning grades to essays filled with mistakes, he returns them ungraded and leads the class through the revision process as an instructional tool. He identifies common errors or misconceptions in student work, delivers targeted minilessons, and guides students to revise their work based on this supplementary instruction.

Providing group feedback in this manner is one way to make the process more efficient. After analyzing student work for recurring misunderstandings, teachers can create a presentation highlighting common issues and offer explanations and clarification. Science teacher Kim Haber uses homework similarly, having students self-correct their homework and discuss answers as a class while Kim emphasizes the value of learning from mistakes. This approach prioritizes students showing their work and thought processes over getting the right answer. "Mistakes are welcome in the classroom," Kim says. "We don't grade based on how many answers they got correct." Mistakes—and the willingness of students to make them—are crucial to the learning process (Matteucci et al., 2024; Soncini et al., 2022).

Try to limit your efforts to giving detailed feedback only on work that students can revise, with a focus on a few key points that they can improve on. Consistently ask yourself, "Is this feedback actionable?" Evaluative feedback after a task rarely leads to improved performance on subsequent assessments (Schinske & Tanner, 2014). Students have little incentive to revisit their work once a grade has been recorded and the class has moved on. To counter this issue, build in opportunities for students to revise and resubmit their work based on your feedback. This encourages them to engage with your comments and fosters ongoing improvement.

Physics teacher Brennan Brockback combines learning progressions with opportunities to revise work in class, resulting in a dynamic feedback loop where students drive their own learning and grade improvement. This type of iterative process empowers students, giving them a tangible sense of control over their academic outcomes and reinforcing a growth mindset. Brennan remarks, "I provide targeted feedback on lab work and students implement improvements. It's a more worthwhile form of practice." Such an approach transforms routine assignments into meaningful learning experiences and prepares learners to demonstrate their knowledge and skills on more formally assessed tasks.

Ongoing formative assessment leveraging detailed feedback helps identify and correct misconceptions throughout the learning process and ensures students have a solid understanding of key concepts before facing summative or performance assessments. Instead of solely focusing on correcting errors, help students learn from their mistakes. Error correction tends to stifle learning, whereas learning from mistakes encourages risk taking and fosters an environment where mistakes are seen as opportunities for growth. Overly corrective feedback can lead students to narrowly seek out "correct" answers rather than deepening their understanding (Narciss & Alemdag, 2024).

Just-in-Time Feedback

History teacher Emily Longnecker provides written feedback when called for, but it's not the only way she guides learners. "I am no longer tethered to my desk, writing comments and inputting grades," she says. "Instead, I move around the classroom, engaging with students during discussions and group work." The reduced burden allows Emily to focus on observing and supporting students during their learning process, which has also led to higher-quality interactions with her students. She provides immediate feedback in real time and offers suggestions for improvement while students are actively engaged with the content. Emily's movement primarily enhances student learning, which contrasts with traditional preservice training that often emphasized using proximity to enforce compliance and keep students on task. Her approach, inspired by the Japanese practice of *kikan-shidō* (teaching between the desks), focuses on using movement as a tool to support and engage learners, rather than as a behavior management technique.

Implementing feedback as part of assessment is more than just providing comments; students need time to understand and apply the suggestions. Without this time, feedback risks becoming "dangling data"—given but unused—which overlooks a vital component of the feedback cycle (Sadler, 1989).

Feedback should serve as a guide, helping students bridge gaps in their learning and take the next step in their understanding.

Art teacher Eric Jensen provides students in his jewelry-making class with feedback based on clear product criteria (e.g., soldering skills) that is immediately applicable to their next iteration. For example, he holds up a student's design to show them exactly where improvements are needed. He sits with students and discusses strengths and areas for improvement, transforming feedback from one-way communication to a conversation—an interactive, ongoing process that directly enhances student learning and skill development, creating a more dynamic and effective learning environment.

These teachers have all found valid ways to deepen student learning and improve the assessment process by prioritizing meaningful input over traditional grading. Some focus on identifying trends in student understanding, using this insight to guide targeted reteaching of concepts or skills, transforming assessments into learning tools, and shifting some cognitive load to students. Others provide just-in-time, individualized, targeted, actionable feedback. These are just a few of the ways that implementing an efficient, effective feedback process in the classroom can work to reduce teacher workload, enhance equitable educational practices, and prepare students for the challenges of summative assessments and real-world tasks.

Effective feedback strategies also address equity gaps by providing all students, regardless of their background or resources, with equal opportunities for improvement and growth. Focusing on individual progress and understanding rather than comparative grades creates a level playing field, ensuring that students who may lack support outside the classroom are not disadvantaged. Further, this personalized approach allows teachers to identify and address specific challenges faced by historically underserved students, promoting a more inclusive and equitable learning environment.

Spotlight: Using Feedback to Set Goals
Rachel Veto, Modern Languages, Country Day School
Chestnut Hill, Massachusetts

Rachel Veto has students in her French classes use the feedback she provides to formulate their own learning goals. Rather than leaving detailed feedback on each mistake, she limits it to broader positive comments and suggestions for growth. Students review the suggestions she's given them for each skill area, reflect on them, and use the input to formulate their own learning goals (see Figure 2.1). This process helps students think metacognitively about their learning and identify and invest in steps to take to be successful.

FIGURE 2.1
Using Feedback to Set Student Goals

	Skill Area: Conversation	**Skill Area: Writing**
Positive comments	• You understood your partner and were able to express your opinion on familiar topics. • You incorporated our class discussion and vocabulary words with your own opinions and experience.	• You were able to elaborate on your opinion, using different tenses. • You clearly understood the original material and were able to describe it. • You used a lot of vocabulary words.
Suggestions for growth	• You used a lot of the same verbs and vocabulary words, so think about ways to give more details. • Look for opportunities to discuss the topic over time, which will allow you to elaborate and show more of your skills.	• Pay attention to how you respond to opinions that you disagree with. • Be careful about use of past tense and work on plural verbs and adjectives.
My goals	• I want to work on using different verbs and more vocabulary words. • I want to make sure to incorporate the past tense into my conversation.	• I want to work on cultural awareness by relating to other people and events. • I want to work on past tense and incorporate that better into my writing.

Rachel describes her students as "much less anxious" with this process than traditional grading practices: "Grades are like the water we swim in, but with this approach, my students often express relief. . . . Whenever a student worries about performing poorly on an assessment and asks how it will affect their grade, I explain that there's no way for their grade to decrease. They can only improve by providing better evidence of progress."

This learning-focused approach shifts students' perceptions of success from simply achieving high grades to developing meaningful skills and processes for learning. For example, Rachel observed this transformation in a junior student who enrolled in her advanced French class. At the start of the term, the student's goals were primarily grade-oriented: "I want to get an A in the class. I am very committed to maintaining my GPA." However, by the end of the year, the student's focus had evolved: "After this course ends, I will still be thinking about subjunctive and hypothetical situations because I still think I can understand those topics more. I will stay in touch with my French." This shift illustrates how students become skill-focused lifelong learners, integrating their developing language abilities into their identities.

This year, Rachel is collaborating with others in her department to evaluate the best ways to help students meet academic standards. This includes providing teachers with prepared positive comments and growth suggestion options they can select from drop-down menus or copy and paste, significantly reducing the time needed to craft feedback for a large number of students. Rachel used artificial intelligence (AI) technology to generate initial recommendations and suggestions based on the district's standards, then refined the language to be more appropriate for middle school students and fine-tuned suggestions to align with learning targets. Teachers in the department personalize the feedback for their students, which in many cases can be as simple as integrating students' names.

This approach will not only save Rachel and her colleagues valuable time but also ensure consistency in feedback across the department while still allowing for personalization. Making the feedback process more manageable helps teachers provide more frequent and targeted feedback. Rachel expects to refine the system over time to incorporate new insights and guard against any trends that preclude personalization—ultimately creating an effective resource for supporting student learning that emphasizes skills and understanding rather than scores and grades. Paradoxically, students are then more confident and well prepared for the challenge of summative evaluations when they are presented with them.

Spotlight Questions

- What is your reaction to Rachel's current feedback process? What do you think about her plans for refining and distributing the system?
- How do you help your students reflect on and incorporate feedback? Formulate their own learning goals?
- How does Rachel's spotlight inspire you to refine your own practices?
- How can you collaborate with colleagues to share strategies for shifting the focus of assessment from grades to feedback in your school?

Purposeful, Personalized Feedback

Although multitasking is popular today, as teachers, we understand that the human brain can only process a few new things at once, making it crucial that instructional practices focus on specific, attainable learning targets (Sweller, 2022). Setting too many goals can lead to stress and difficulty prioritizing for both teachers and students. Likewise, excessive feedback can overwhelm students and undermine learning objectives. Hattie and Timperley (2007) found that when educators provide too much feedback, students become confused, rendering the feedback ineffective. Therefore, feedback should align closely with focused learning targets.

In addition, effective feedback connects with the recipient. Zaretta Hammond (2015) emphasizes the importance of culturally responsive feedback processes and developing a "cognitive alliance" with students, particularly in meeting the needs of traditionally marginalized learners. This cognitive alliance, built on a foundation of trust, positions the teacher as an ally in students' next steps in their learning journey. The alliance implies a mutual commitment to effort and facing challenges together. Teachers guide students toward their next developmental stage, and students trust in their teachers' unwavering support, regardless of successes or setbacks (Hammond, 2015). A supportive learning environment encourages growth and resilience, dovetailing with Vygotsky's (1978) zone of proximal development, which describes the range between what learners can do independently and what they can achieve with guidance and encouragement. Teacher–student collaboration is fundamental to this process.

Essential collaboration and communication between teacher and student can be strengthened through one-on-one consultation, although we should note that some traditional scenarios for meeting with students detract from the goals of equity and student learning and should be avoided. For example, out-of-class meetings (before school, during lunch, or after school) may be perceived by students as punitive, which can damage the teacher–student relationship and hinder effective communication. Such arrangements can also disadvantage students who lack personal transportation, rely on school-provided meals during lunch periods, or have family responsibilities or part-time jobs outside school hours.

Middle school math teacher Sara Daley has a conference with each of her students after the first assessment of the year, providing them with "very specific things to do when they walk away from the meeting." She ensures each student leaves the session with clear, actionable steps for improvement. Although it may seem daunting to make time for individual conferences with each student, there are other ways to offer personalized feedback, guidance, and support to students that may integrate into what you are already doing.

Project-Based Learning and the Workshop Model

Project-based learning classrooms naturally allow for structured one-on-one consultations while other student teams or individuals work on projects. The workshop model, in which teachers present a minilesson followed by student-centered individual or small-group work before coming back together as a class to debrief, also provides an ideal setting for one-on-one consultations. As students engage in the workshop phase, teachers can circulate among small groups, assessing progress and offering immediate guidance. They may also seize the opportunity to conduct brief individual consultations and provide personalized feedback and targeted instruction, enhancing students' learning while maintaining class momentum.

Flex Days, Makeup Days, and Review Days

Schools with built-in "flex" periods where students and teachers are released from official classes (e.g., once or twice weekly) can allow this time to be used for teacher–student consultations. Instead of tutoring or proctoring retake exams, teachers can meet individually with students to discuss their progress, offer feedback, and set a student's next learning steps together.

Many teachers already schedule "makeup days," offering unstructured time for students to catch up on their assignments. These days can be repurposed to schedule individual meetings to clarify progress, discuss feedback, and co-construct improvement goals. While the teacher is conferring with individual students, the rest of the class could, for example, engage in an in-depth exploration of topics related to their studies.

Online Breakout Rooms

In distance-learning scenarios, teachers can use online breakout rooms for small-group or individual consultations, providing a virtual space for personalized interaction. Breakout groups might cluster students based on their needs to more efficiently differentiate for a small number of learners.

Honing Learning Intentions

For maximum benefit, a shift to focusing on students using feedback to improve learning outcomes must be accompanied by an emphasis on student goal setting. Nancie Atwell's (1987) Status of the Class strategy is a versatile technique that works across content areas, grade levels, and types of independent work. The approach starts with students taking a moment at the beginning of each work period to independently reflect and set specific goals (the teacher can scaffold this process with a checklist of requirements or learning targets). The teacher then asks each student to commit to their goal, recording these commitments in a Status of the Class document, which serves as a reference for the teacher as they circulate and check on individual progress (see Figure 2.2). Typically, the entire process of asking for and recording the status of the class takes about 90 seconds, making it an efficient yet powerful tool for enhancing student engagement and accountability.

Tracking Feedback and Progress

Monitoring students' engagement with formative assessment can provide insights into their learning processes and readiness for summative evaluations. Patterns between participation in practice tasks and performance on

FIGURE 2.2
Sample Status of the Class Document

Period 3 Students	October 7 Review Day	October 8 Workshop
Alberto	Rewatch ecosystem module.	Read summary of investigation.
Bennie	Review lab notes and make concept map.	Write the investigation steps.
Clara	Take the preview quiz on ecosystems.	Work with group on habitat ecology scenarios.
Kendra	Rewatch aquatic ecosystem module.	Work with group on Venn diagram of freshwater lake-to-pond systems.
Maura	Meet with teacher.	Implement redo ideas for investigation.
Sam	Take the preview quiz on terrestrial systems.	Work with team to decide which subsystems to investigate (forest, etc.).

graded assessments can reveal correlations that indicate whether a student is prepared for retakes or additional evaluation. Tracking patterns can also inform decisions about when to time retakes or recommend completion of other graded tasks, ensuring that students have adequately engaged with the learning material before attempting summative assessments. However, it's crucial to maintain a clear distinction between tracking these activities for instructional purposes and grading them, as the latter can undermine the intended role of formative assessment in the learning process and potentially produce inequalities among students.

Regardless of how feedback is communicated to students, tracking the information exchanged is crucial (and prevents the frustration of repeatedly providing the same feedback to students). Many teachers use physical or digital notebooks to track the types of feedback each student receives. These notebooks serve multiple purposes: They help teachers monitor each student's developmental progress, act as a reference during individual conferences, and hold students accountable for previous feedback. Typically, a teacher notebook includes a dedicated page or section for each student.

In a typical conference, the teacher and student collaboratively identify a success related to the learning target and set a specific goal (including details on how the student will achieve it), and the teacher notes the feedback provided. This ensures that feedback is effectively used and built on over time, fostering continuous improvement and personalized learning experiences for each student.

Both teacher and student should maintain parallel tracking systems for monitoring progress. During conferences, each refers to their respective page, ensuring that the same information is recorded and discussed (see Figure 2.3). Students typically keep their tracking pages in their class notebooks or alongside their practice work and notes. This collaborative conference approach allows students to acknowledge their successes and provides them with a clear plan for improvement. By the end of the conference, students feel a sense of accomplishment about their progress and have a concrete strategy for further growth. This system fosters a sense of ownership in the learning process and ensures that teacher and student are aligned in their understanding of the student's development and next steps.

Feedback practices such as we've discussed here break down the learning process into small, manageable segments with deadlines and check-ins, replacing the traditional single due date for all work. This structure facilitates continuous exchange, allowing students to refine their work incrementally. Implementing checkpoints has multiple benefits. Short-term progress goals are consistently met, students maintain steady advancement in their projects, and the tendency to procrastinate is significantly reduced. Students are less likely to rush through assignments at the last minute, resulting in more thoughtful and polished final products and demonstration of learning. This system not only enhances the learning experience but also cultivates time management skills that extend beyond the classroom while actively combating inequities in education.

FIGURE 2.3
Sample Teacher and Student Notebook Pages

Teacher Notebook	
October 8	
Success	Kendra included factual evidence to support the claim.
Goal	Add a direct quote to support the claim or paraphrased information from the text.
Feedback or plan	Feedback focused on the rubric, as well as talking through one example related to the text.
October 15	
Success	Kendra added one direct quote and one paraphrased piece of evidence to support the claim.
Goal	Work on citations; join a peer editing group to smooth out the connections between added evidence and each paragraph.
Feedback or plan	Feedback provided examples of citations and suggestions for members of peer editing group.

Student Notebook	
October 8	
Success	I included factual evidence to support the claim.
Goal	Add direct quote or paraphrased info from text.
Feedback or plan	Look at rubric and provided example.
October 15	
Success	Added a quote and one piece of paraphrased info from text.
Goal	Work on citations and fluency with the new evidence and the words I already had.
Feedback or plan	Review examples of citations and meet with peer editing group during workshop time tomorrow.

Providing frequent, targeted feedback and multiple opportunities for improvement levels the playing field for students who may lack resources or support outside school. The incremental nature of the work allows for early intervention and support, preventing students from falling behind due to external factors, and ensures that students who need more time to grasp concepts are not penalized. The emphasis on process over product reduces the effects of socioeconomic disparities on academic performance, as success is measured by growth and persistence rather than access to resources. By improving students' ability to manage their time, this approach equips all students with essential life skills, potentially breaking cycles of disadvantage. Ultimately, these practices create a more inclusive learning environment where all students, regardless of their background, have equitable opportunities to succeed and demonstrate their learning.

Technologies to Support Efficient Feedback

Integrating technology such as AI and educational games into the feedback process for student learning presents both opportunities and significant challenges, especially in promoting critical thinking skills. These tools offer immediate feedback at scale, providing students with real-time insights into their performance and areas for improvement (Hawlitschek, 2017). The engaging nature of educational games can increase student motivation and participation; AI-powered systems can adapt to individual learning needs, ensuring students are consistently challenged at an appropriate level (Chen et al., 2020).

However, the use of these technologies is not without limitations. There's a risk of overreliance on AI-generated feedback, potentially hindering students' development of self-assessment skills (Spector & Ma, 2019). AI systems may struggle to capture nuances of learning that teachers can readily identify, and they are less effective at fostering complex problem-solving abilities in students. Ethical concerns around data privacy and algorithmic bias also need careful consideration. Because AI formulates its responses based on data it pulls from numerous internet sources, teachers need to be cautious about the quality and validity of the information provided. AI may generate content based on outdated, biased, or inaccurate data, potentially spreading misinformation if not critically evaluated, which underscores the importance of human oversight and the need to verify AI-generated content against reliable sources.

To maximize benefits while mitigating limitations, teachers should view these technologies as supplements to, rather than replacements for, human instruction. AI-powered feedback systems should encourage reflection and self-assessment, incorporating open-ended questions that require students to apply knowledge in novel contexts (Lamb et al., 2018).

Let's say you would like to use an AI-powered feedback tool to provide initial feedback on student essays. After students receive the AI-generated comments, ask them to highlight areas with which they agree or disagree, and then discuss in small groups the AI's suggestions, its accuracy, and its usefulness. You might also have students write a brief reflection addressing (1) which AI suggestions they plan to incorporate and why, (2) feedback they disagree with and their reasoning, and (3) additional areas of improvement they've identified that the AI missed. This student reflection can then provide a basis for personalized guidance from you (in one-on-one conferences or groups) as well as classwide reflections or attributes that may inform your teaching.

A systematic approach such as this leverages AI's efficiency while promoting critical thinking, self-assessment, and personalized instruction. It also helps students develop the important skill of evaluating feedback from various sources, encouraging them to question and verify information. It maintains a necessary balance between technological and human interaction, providing opportunities for peer feedback and collaborative problem solving. This not only leverages the advantages of technology but also nurtures the essential critical thinking skills students need for success.

As AI tools become more adept at generating polished written work, an increasing number of students are turning to these technologies not just to receive feedback but to compose entire essays. This shift poses a significant challenge for educators committed to developing authentic student writing skills. In response, many teachers are now placing greater emphasis on in-class writing, reflections, and assessments—contexts in which students must rely on their own abilities rather than the cognitive horsepower of the machine. By creating more opportunities for students to write independently, teachers aim to ensure that feedback remains genuine and that essential elements of the writing process, such as idea development and personal voice, are not outsourced to AI.

AI and other technology tools may help create a more engaging and effective learning environment. However, it is essential to remain mindful of potential drawbacks and to continually assess the influence of these technologies on students' critical thinking skills and overall learning outcomes (Guo & Ji, 2019). This is especially true when considering the nature of the teacher–student relationship and cognitive alliance. The goal should be to harness the power of AI and educational games to enhance rather than replace the pivotal role of educators in fostering critical thinking and comprehensive learning.

There are also valid concerns about inequitable access to technology, also known as the "digital divide." Rushing into implementing new technologies can exacerbate existing inequalities and hinder the academic success of students whose households lack reliable internet connections and up-to-date technology. For a recent illustration of this, recall that many school districts struggled to address issues relating to asynchronous learning over the internet during the COVID-19 pandemic. To ensure equitable access, educators and policymakers must consider all components of digital equity: motivation and positive attitude, physical access to study spaces, devices and internet, digital skills, and accessible tools. If these aspects of technology use are not addressed comprehensively, the integration of AI and educational games may widen achievement gaps.

Feedback as Part of a Classroom Culture

Classroom culture can either center on the teacher as sole expert or distribute expertise across the learning environment. Student autonomy is crucial for effective learning, which includes developing students' abilities to self-assess (Andrade & Brookhart, 2020; McMillan & Hearn, 2008) and provide peer feedback (Deci & Ryan, 2000). To foster these skills, exercises in goal setting and reflection can help students learn to compare their work against established criteria (Heritage, 2007). Developing individual and collective reflective skills not only enhances students' metacognitive abilities but also creates a more collaborative and empowering learning environment where expertise is shared among all participants.

Although most educators would like students to naturally assess their learning and progress toward educational goals, the reality is that our fast-paced instruction often leaves little room for such reflection. Teachers must intentionally incorporate reflection time within class sessions. Teaching reflection skills helps shift students from a dependent mindset, where they passively await feedback from the teacher, to one of independence and ownership over the learning process. Deliberately creating opportunities for reflection empowers students to actively engage with their own progress and development.

Model a Growth Mindset

Demonstrating and encouraging language that reflects continuous learning and improvement in the classroom supports the development of a growth mindset. For example, when introducing a new concept, share a personal anecdote about your own learning journey with that topic. Use phrases like "I'm still working on understanding . . ." or "This is challenging, but I'm excited to keep improving." Encourage students to reframe their struggles as opportunities for growth, and celebrate effort and progress rather than just final outcomes. This focus encourages all students, regardless of their background, to believe in their capacity for improvement and helps counteract the effects of socioeconomic status on student achievement.

Showcase Student Thinking

Having students share their work and explain their thought processes fosters peer learning and self-reflection. Consider dedicating time in each lesson for a "student spotlight," in which a volunteer or selected student presents their work. Guide the presenter with questions that prompt them to articulate their thinking, such as "What was your approach to solving this problem?" or "How did you decide on this particular strategy?" Encourage respectful peer questions and feedback to deepen the learning experience for all, a practice that provides opportunities for all voices to be heard and valued, promoting a sense of belonging for all students.

Guide Reflection with Prompts

Provide students with structured reflection questions or sentence frames, such as "One thing I did well was . . ." or "One thing I am still learning is. . . ." Integrate these prompts into daily or weekly routines, perhaps as exit tickets or journal entries. Gradually increase the complexity of the prompts as students become more comfortable with self-reflection. For instance, progress from simple statements to more analytical questions such as "How does this new learning connect to what I already know? What strategies were most effective for me in this task, and why?" This approach helps students develop the metacognitive skills essential for long-term academic success.

Facilitate Collaborative Assessment

To build student skills in evaluating work (their own and that of others) against assessment criteria, begin by modeling the process as a class. Present examples of student work at various stages of learning, guide students in comparing the samples with established criteria, and have them suggest next steps for the authors to meet those criteria. Next, have students take "gallery walks" of anonymized work samples ranging from emerging to proficient levels. Provide them with a rubric or checklist to guide them in analyzing each sample and leaving constructive feedback on sticky notes. Conclude the activity with a class discussion about common strengths, areas for improvement, and effective strategies observed. This practice exposes students to different perspectives and approaches, fostering cultural competence and reducing bias.

You can then gradually release responsibility to student groups (Fisher & Frey, 2021), providing clear guidelines for respectful and constructive feedback. Rotate roles within groups so students can be both assessor and presenter, and conclude collaborative sessions with a whole-class debrief in which groups share their insights and reflect on the assessment process. This kind of student collaboration encourages peer learning and develops important interpersonal skills.

Together, these methods create a more equitable classroom environment by acknowledging diverse learning needs, reducing bias, providing multiple opportunities for success, and fostering engagement and motivation among all students—ultimately working toward closing achievement gaps and promoting equity in education. These strategies also provide students with the practice and confidence necessary to do their best on summative assessments.

Peer Assessment

Band teacher Collin Stegner consistently seeks to enhance his students' use of feedback, and he believes in the value of receiving feedback not just from an instructor but from one's peers. His school has a high population of multilingual learners, and Collin's primary goal is to develop independent, collaborative students. He achieves this by providing scaffolded opportunities for all students to engage in the feedback process. Collin emphasizes, "I'm constantly thinking about how to make things better for my students. Building a supportive classroom culture is key. It enhances their learning while reducing teacher workload."

To foster collaboration, each section of the band listens to recordings of their performances and sets improvement goals as a section. They use academic language from the classroom word wall (e.g., *melody, harmony, tempo, dynamics*), which is particularly beneficial for multilingual learners. The student-developed goals include ways to measure progress, such as "We will play in tune across the full range of our instruments at various dynamic levels by the end of the semester" or "We will demonstrate proficiency in these rhythmic patterns through scale studies, technical exercises, and ensemble performance." Collin then circulates during class rehearsals, providing feedback on their practice. This group goal-setting and practice approach improves each section's performance as well as enhancing the whole band's performance at their concert—in effect, their collective summative assessment.

Developing students' skills in peer feedback is a gradual process that requires time and practice. Teachers can begin with low-stakes feedback exercises to help students become comfortable with giving and receiving constructive comments. A common starting point is the compliment-and-question strategy, where student partners provide each other with one compliment and one thoughtful question. As students grow more confident with this process, teachers can introduce a third element, in which students offer a suggestion linked to assessment criteria.

By taking a slow, step-by-step approach and consistently modeling effective feedback techniques, teachers create an environment where students can successfully engage in peer assessment. Gradual implementation allows students to build confidence and competence in providing helpful, constructive feedback to their peers. Teachers can support this development in several ways.

Clarify Learning Objectives

Help students focus by clearly defining and communicating the goals of the assignment or task. You might start each lesson or unit by explicitly stating the learning objectives. Write them on the board, project them, or provide them in a handout. Use student-friendly language and explain how these objectives relate to the broader course goals. Encourage students to recast the learning targets in their own words and to refer to these objectives throughout the learning process.

Demonstrate Effective Feedback

Use an exemplar to model how to provide feedback that directly addresses the established criteria. You might select a sample piece of work from a previous student or one you've created and walk through the feedback process as a class. Show students how to identify strengths and areas for improvement based on the learning objectives. Use specific, descriptive language and avoid general praise or criticism.

Provide a Structured Approach

Offer clear guidelines and sentence frames to guide students in giving constructive feedback to their peers. One method to implement this approach is to create a feedback form or rubric that aligns with the learning objectives (see Chapter 3). Teach students how to use these tools effectively, emphasizing the importance of specific, actionable feedback.

Allow for Clarification

Allocate time for feedback recipients to ask questions, ensuring they understand how to implement the suggestions they've received. Consider setting aside dedicated periods after feedback sessions for students to review and reflect on feedback. Encourage them to ask clarifying questions and discuss potential strategies for improvement. This can be done in small groups or in one-on-one student–teacher conferences.

Benefits of Feedback on Formative Tasks

Effective feedback on formative tasks can significantly enhance student performance on summative assessments and other high-stakes graded tasks. Providing clear, timely, actionable feedback during the learning process helps students identify their strengths and areas for improvement before a culminating assessment. Strategies such as aligning feedback with learning objectives, offering process-level feedback, and encouraging self-reflection help students develop a deeper understanding of the material and improve their metacognitive skills—and they will approach summative exams or performances with greater confidence and competence.

Regular formative feedback creates a culture of continuous improvement and reduces the anxiety often associated with higher-stakes demonstrations of learning (i.e., performance for grades). Focusing on growth and learning helps motivate students to engage with the material and apply the feedback they receive. The ongoing process of feedback and improvement helps students develop better study habits, critical thinking skills, and self-regulation strategies, all of which contribute to improved performance on culminating assessments. Using different feedback methods such as peer feedback and self-assessment helps students internalize evaluation criteria and develop a more nuanced understanding of what constitutes high-quality work, further preparing them for success in their displays of mastery or proficiency.

Creating a Culture Shift

A culture shift requires time and persistence. In many schools, there is an ingrained culture of grade seeking. Students begin receiving grades in upper elementary school, and by middle or high school they've become deeply acclimated to the grading system. Sergio López, a Spanish language teacher notes,

> Students ask, "What does this mean? Did I get an A or a B?" Or they want to know exactly what percentage they received. And so you have to train them over time to not focus on the letter grade and instead focus on the feedback and on developing the skills and what area to work on instead of the grade.

To shift students' focus from grade seeking to using feedback for improvement, teachers need to provide guidance for interpreting and acting on feedback, distilling for students the meaning behind rubric scores or written comments and how to identify next steps. Once students learn to interpret feedback constructively, they can apply it to improve their work and deepen their learning journey. Transitioning from a grade focus to feedback focus is crucial to fostering a growth mindset and promoting continuous improvement.

Students may initially struggle with accepting and using feedback, especially if your classroom is their first experience with receiving actionable guidance coupled with encouragement for improvement. Embracing a growth mindset involves not only acknowledging mistakes but also actively using them as learning opportunities. This requires a shift in perspective for both teachers and students. As Vatterott (2015) aptly states, "If we expect students to take ownership of their learning, we must accept the fact that learning is not error-free. Mistakes will be made during learning" (p. 51).

By fostering an environment where mistakes are viewed as stepping-stones to improvement rather than failures, we can help students become more receptive to feedback and more invested in their own learning process. Students with a growth mindset who are more invested in their learning will develop resilience, curiosity, and continuous growth, ultimately leading to becoming more effective and engaged learners. A world languages teacher we've worked with puts it this way:

> One thing I really love is the shift I see in students' perspectives over the course of the year. At the beginning, when I survey them about why they're taking the class, most say things like, "I just want to get an A" or "I need it for college." But by the end of the year, their responses change dramatically. They start saying things like "I want to travel," "I want to meet new people," or "I want to explore different places." This transformation is extremely satisfying because it shows that the focus has shifted from merely achieving a grade to embracing lifelong learning.

Pause and Reflect

Take a look at the following prompts and select a couple that are relevant to you based on where you are in shifting students' focus from grade seeking to using feedback to improve their learning. Reflect on your own, discuss with colleagues one-on-one, or start a discussion with your team.

- Reflect on your current practices for helping students use feedback effectively, beyond focusing on scores or grades. What strategies have you found successful? Which new ideas from this chapter do you plan to incorporate into your approach?

- How can you enhance your current methods to more actively involve students in both giving and receiving constructive feedback to improve their work?
- Which method for organizing one-on-one teacher–student feedback consultations particularly interests you, and why?
- To what extent are your colleagues already addressing the separation of feedback from grades as discussed in this chapter? What specific topic related to this issue would you like to introduce or further explore in conversations with them?

3

Rubrics and Progress Tracking

Breaking Down Barriers to Grade Transparency

Have you ever felt blindsided by an exam grade, realizing there was a disconnect between your study efforts and what the test focused on? This common and frustrating experience reflects an educational environment where learning targets are unclear and preparing for assessments feels like a guessing game. Our students deserve better than that. But what are the best ways to help them understand what they need to learn to succeed on a summative assessment?

Traditional grading practices are prone to bias and inaccuracy. Subjectivity can lead to inconsistencies in grading, and factors unrelated to academic performance can influence grades (Feldman, 2019b; Robbins, 2025). A lack of transparency perpetuates inequities in education and compromises the validity of a grade as a measure of true student learning, rewarding those who "crack the code" of teacher expectations over those who genuinely master the material.

Rubrics and student trackers have emerged as powerful tools to address these challenges and promote more equitable grading practices. Rubrics identify specific skills and knowledge that students need to achieve for various levels of proficiency, and trackers help students understand how their skills and knowledge measure up.

It's important to note that efforts by teachers to track student progress can inadvertently sideline student reflection and goal setting, crucial aspects of the learning process. When teachers take on the bulk of progress tracking, they miss opportunities to foster student agency and independence (Panadero & Jönsson, 2013). This is why we are placing an emphasis on students keeping track of their own progress toward the goals they set for themselves.

Transparent grading rubrics and student-friendly tracking systems not only increase students' ownership of their learning—a hallmark of equitable assessment—but also allow teachers to focus on instruction and feedback. In fact, involving students in the rubric creation process can deepen their understanding and increase buy-in, and empowering students to track their own progress toward competency transforms the learning experience from one of passive reception to active engagement (Panadero & Romero, 2014).

By harnessing the full potential of rubrics, educators can create more equitable and transparent grading practices that bridge the gaps between instruction, assessment, and student understanding. These efforts help transform practice work and assessments from sources of stress into powerful tools for learning and equitable evaluation, fostering an environment where all students can thrive.

Pitfalls of the 100-Point Scale

Before examining the design and use of rubrics and student trackers as a more effective and equitable approach to grading, we need to critically evaluate the status quo for schools across the country: the 100-point grading scale. The 100-point grading scale has been a cornerstone of the U.S. education system for more than 150 years. Originally designed as a ranking system, the scale was never intended to assess students' knowledge and skills related to essential learning objectives (Feldman, 2019b). Despite its deep-rooted presence in our shared educational experience, the scale is arbitrary and, when used as a measurement tool, proves both clumsy and inaccurate in gauging a student's learning trajectory or informing a teacher's next steps.

The scale presents significant pitfalls in assessing student learning, particularly in its bias toward failure, which stems from the mathematical imbalance that disproportionately affects scores below 50 (Reeves, 2004). Whereas passing grades (typically 60–100) span only 40 points, failing grades (0–59) span 60 points, creating an uneven distribution that gives failing grades much more influence on a student's overall average.

O'Connor (2011) highlights one of the most problematic aspects of this scale: the use of zeros. Zeros disproportionately affect disadvantaged students and create a mathematical imbalance that is often insurmountable, leading to student disengagement. A zero rarely represents a student's actual knowledge or skills—it most frequently indicates missing work—yet it has a catastrophic effect on their overall grade. A student who receives a zero needs to score 100 on two additional assignments just to achieve a C average, making recovery from a single low score extremely challenging (Guskey, 2015). Many students struggle at the start of a term with a curriculum that is new to them, then quickly realize how deep a hole they are in. As a result, they disengage, much to the consternation of the teacher who might not fully understand how their grading framework is undermining student motivation.

Moreover, the 100-point scale creates an illusion of precision that is not supported by assessment realities. Whereas grading scales with four to seven levels provide optimal distinction among different levels of performance, as well as ensuring validity and reliability in grading (Brookhart, 2011), the excessive gradations of the 100-point scale lead to greater subjectivity, increased errors, and diminished reliability in assessing student work. If you've ever found yourself faced with a frustrated student who feels their 89 should really be a 90 (to make it an A-instead of a B) or one beseeching you for a couple more points needed to reach a 60 to pass the class, you may have questioned the reliability of this process yourself.

The practice of averaging scores over a grading period further compounds these issues by blending unequal representations of learning and undervaluing student growth. These systemic flaws not only affect students' academic records but also inflict damage on their motivation, self-worth, and approach to learning, ultimately perpetuating education inequities (Feldman, 2019b).

A Path to Accurate, Equitable Grading

Rubrics and rubric-based tracking systems offer an alternative to traditional 100-point or percentage-based grading scales. Using rubrics, educators can focus on specific skills and competencies, applying credible performance markers rather than arbitrary numerical cutoffs (Brookhart, 2018). Well-designed rubrics offer increased accuracy and specificity in assessment by providing clear, detailed criteria for performance levels. This gives students a better understanding of what is expected of them and how they can improve (Jönsson & Panadero, 2017). Rubrics make expectations for high-quality work visible and give students a road map to satisfy these expectations. In this way, rubrics also support students who may lack the background knowledge to intuitively understand what constitutes "good work," leveling the playing field for students from diverse backgrounds and experiences.

Although rubrics offer immense potential for advancing equitable grading practices, implementing them in the classroom does have its challenges (Taylor et al., 2024). Creating rubrics entails identifying essential standards, embedding clear learning targets in teaching, and finding time to co-construct these tools with students or colleagues—balanced with the constant demands of teaching. Rubrics also are not a one-size-fits-all solution; their effectiveness is dependent upon careful consideration and thoughtful implementation. Rubrics need to be integrated into a broader assessment strategy, complementing other forms of feedback and instruction, and students need to learn how to interpret and use them effectively.

Rubric Design

Rubrics describe qualitative differences in student performance across multiple dimensions of learning. Unlike the arbitrary precision of percentage grades, rubrics typically establish three to five performance levels with distinct, meaningful labels such as "novice," "developing," "proficient," and "exceeds proficiency." By focusing on specific learning outcomes and skills rather than numerical scores, rubrics allow for more consistent evaluation of student work regardless of who is assessing the work. Breaking complex tasks into specific, clear criteria allows educators to evaluate both tangible skills and abstract abilities and provides a more comprehensive and nuanced understanding of student achievement than relying solely on a single percentage grade. Such an approach not only enhances the fairness and consistency of grading but also shifts the focus from assigning arbitrary point values to evaluating learning outcomes in a meaningful way, ultimately supporting more equitable assessment practices.

Identifying Essential Standards

The first step in constructing an effective rubric is identifying the essential standards being assessed. Essential standards represent the critical learning outcomes that students must master. Effective rubrics draw from these standards to offer clear guidance for both teachers and students. Many teachers have little experience with breaking down standards into discrete, measurable skills or tracking student progress on specific standards over a semester. Katherine Holden, a former Oregon middle school teacher, recalled that when teachers were asked to monitor progress across three standards, many struggled. "Was there maybe something in your gradebook that should be able to validate whether they're proficient or not on what you were teaching throughout the year?" This discomfort motivated teachers to realize the need to better define their criteria.

Some educators must sift through numerous state and national standards to determine which are truly essential. This time-consuming culling process can feel overwhelming and requires careful consideration and collaboration among teaching teams. When Rachel Veto's Modern Languages department undertook a comprehensive process to identify essential standards for their courses, they first created an extensive list, then identified overlaps and related concepts, and finally distilled the list into focused learning targets for each course. These learning targets were then used to inform daily lesson plans and develop assessment rubrics, balancing key curricular areas and enhancing teacher and student understanding of learning objectives. Although it may feel daunting to choose, researchers emphasize that focusing on a limited number of essential standards allows for deeper learning, prevents superficial coverage of topics, and ensures students develop meaningful understanding and mastery of the most important concepts (Reeves, 2006; Schmoker, 2018).

The process of essential standard identification should include the following important steps:

- **Apply objective selection criteria and focus on comprehensive standards.** Categorize the standards according to REAL criteria (*r*eadiness, *e*ndurance, *a*ssessed, *l*everage). *Readiness* standards prepare students for the next level of learning. *Endurance* standards focus on knowledge and skills that remain relevant throughout students' academic careers and beyond. *Assessed* standards are those that are likely to be evaluated on high-stakes tests or are important in the broader curriculum. *Leverage* standards are those that apply across multiple disciplines. Prioritize rigorous standards encompassing broader concepts over foundational ones.

For instance, in math, emphasize problem-solving skills over computational competencies.
- **Collaborate with colleagues.** Grade-level and subject-area teams should work together to select initial priority standards, ensuring consensus and alignment. Such collaboration helps identify those that are truly essential across different classrooms. Seek input from case managers or special educators to verify that identified standards dovetail with personalized support, tailored interventions, and consistent progress monitoring, maximizing all students' potential for success.
- **Examine the standards for vertical alignment.** Evaluate the standards chosen across grade levels to ensure coherence and progression, avoiding gaps or unnecessary repetition in the curriculum. Remember to account for high-stakes assessments and external exam requirements when selecting essential standards, ensuring students' preparedness for such evaluations. Discuss and plan for any gaps between grade levels that might result from prioritizing certain standards to maintain curriculum continuity.
- **Take student knowledge and needs into account.** Plan for potential learning gaps due to disruptions when selecting essential standards to make sure that students will have the necessary background knowledge. For each selected standard, identify the core content needed to demonstrate mastery, focusing instruction on the most critical aspects.
- **Plan for acceleration.** Emphasize accelerating learning rather than remediation so students can catch up without falling further behind in current grade-level content. Research shows that Black and Latino students are often underrepresented in advanced coursework, even when these classes are available (Patrick et al., 2020). This underrepresentation is due not to lack of ability but rather to systemic barriers and biases. Overreliance on remediation can exacerbate inequities by trapping students in a cycle of low expectations and limited learning opportunities. Teachers with an unconscious deficit lens focus lessons on "the basics" instead of allowing students to undertake grade-level (let alone advanced) curriculum. A focus on remediation can widen achievement gaps as students miss out on the rich, engaging content that could spark their interest and accelerate their learning. Focusing on acceleration and

providing access to rigorous, culturally relevant curriculum promotes a growth mindset and ensures that all students have opportunities to engage in deeper learning experiences that boost their cognitive capacity and long-term academic gains.

Defining the Criteria for the Rubric

Effective rubrics clearly communicate expectations and align assessment with learning objectives, streamlining the assessment process. When developing rubrics, identify key performance indicators, establish clear levels of achievement, and craft descriptive language that meaningfully differentiates between performance levels. Following are some guidelines for rubric design and implementation:

- **Use the essential standards to identify specific learning objectives, along with criteria for assessment and levels of mastery.** For example, in a writing class, "effectively uses evidence to support arguments" may be a key standard, for which the criteria evaluated might include "clearly states the argument," "integration of quotes," and "analysis of evidence."
- **Use student-friendly language.** "Utilizes sophisticated syntax," a description drawn from a curriculum standards document, can be phrased as "uses varied and complex sentence structures." Instead of "demonstrates analysis of the text by synthesizing multiple perspectives and drawing conclusions supported by relevant textual evidence," a more student-friendly version could read "combines different viewpoints from the text to create understanding and backs up ideas with strong examples from the story."
- **Write clear, specific descriptors for each level of performance for each criterion.** A four-level rubric might use Beginning, Developing, Proficient, and Exemplary levels of mastery. For "integration of quotes" at the Proficient level, the descriptor might be "smoothly incorporates quotes using appropriate signal phrases and context." Include a range of performance indicators and a parallel structure across the levels. For a research project, a Beginning descriptor might be "relies on a single source," whereas Exemplary could be "synthesizes information from multiple, diverse sources."
- **Start small.** Begin by implementing rubrics in one unit or assignment, then gradually expand their use as you gain experience and support.

A phased-in process can help alleviate concerns about drastic changes in assessment practices. You might also test the rubric on sample work or with colleagues. Try calibrating assessment by scoring the same student work sample with multiple teachers to check for consistency in interpretation.
- **Align the rubric with grading practices and revise as necessary.** If grammar is less important than content in your grading scheme, ensure it carries less weight in the rubric scoring. Revise the rubric based on feedback and actual use. If students consistently misunderstand a criterion, reword it for clarity. Continual rubric refinement ensures ongoing improvement and alignment with standards throughout the teaching cycle, enhancing the ability to accurately assess student learning.

Phased Implementation

Much like teaching and learning itself, rubric development is an ongoing, iterative process that requires continuous reflection and refinement. At one high school in Washington state, the implementation of rubrics began with the school leadership team examining test data and noticing that, across the board, most students were struggling with writing. They decided to start addressing the challenge by developing a simple, single-point rubric to use across classes and grade levels to support students in meeting writing standards. A single-point rubric sets out the criteria that describe work at a Proficient level and includes space on either side of the criteria for the teacher to note areas for improvement and ways the work exceeds expectations (see Figure 3.1).

The next step in the school's phased implementation was to expand and refine the rubric to describe a spectrum of performance levels and link the criteria to state standards. The faculty worked collaboratively to roll out a more comprehensive, analytic rubric using the same criteria (organization, evidence and reasoning, language use, and conventions) but with a more detailed representation of four performance levels—Emerging, Developing, Proficient, and Exceeds Expectations. Figure 3.2 presents the refined rubric.

We want to stress that using labels instead of numbers to denote levels of performance offers several advantages for both students and instructors.

FIGURE 3.1
Example of a Single-Point Rubric

	Writing Rubric: *One Rubric for the Whole School* Student Name: _____ Grade: _____	
Not Yet	**Proficient**	**Rockin' It**
	Disciplinary-specific purpose: *[filled in by teacher]*	
	Organization • Clear and logical beginning, middle, and end • Clear introduction and conclusion • Uses transitions • Contains central idea/main idea/claim/topic and/or thesis statement	
	Evidence and reasoning • Develops ideas about the topic • Central idea is well supported by evidence (content, background knowledge, or from text) • Includes reasoning that explains the connection of evidence to the topic	
	Language use • Uses content-specific vocabulary suitable to the audience and purpose	
	Conventions • Some errors may be present but do not affect meaning • Adequate, appropriate use of punctuation, capitalization, and spelling	

FIGURE 3.2
Example Analytic Writing Rubric

Criteria	Emerging	Developing	Proficient	Exceeds Expectations
Organization CCSS.ELA-Literacy Standards: ☐ W.11-12.2.A ☐ W.11-12.2 ☐ W.11-12.2.F No evidence: ☐	☐ Introduces an unclear topic ☐ Response lacks logical order ☐ Transitions between ideas are limited ☐ Response ends without conclusion	☐ Introduces clear topic ☐ Inconsistently organizes ideas in a logical sequence ☐ Transitions between ideas can be followed ☐ Conclusion simply restates the main idea	☐ Introduces a clear and compelling topic ☐ Consistently organizes ideas in a logical sequence ☐ Uses appropriate and varied transitions effectively to link major ideas together ☐ Conclusion follows and elaborates on main ideas	☐ Strategically or skillfully transitions to link the major sections of text ☐ Conclusion provides insight to implications, explains significance of topic, and projects to the future

Rubrics and Progress Tracking

Evidence and reasoning CCSS.ELA-Literacy Standards: ☐ W.11-12.1.B ☐ W.11-12.2.B No evidence: ☐	☐ Attempts to develop the topic by including evidence but does not support a central idea ☐ Reasoning does not provide explanation of the connection between evidence and topic	☐ Develops the topic by including evidence that provides limited support for the central idea ☐ Reasoning provides limited explanation of the connection between evidence and topic	☐ Thoroughly develops the topic by including evidence that provides sufficient support for the central idea ☐ Reasoning provides sufficient explanation of the connection between evidence and topic	☐ Thoroughly develops the topic by including a variety of evidence that provides compelling or convincing support for the central idea ☐ Audience concerns, values, and possible biases may be taken into account
Language use CCSS.ELA-Literacy Standards: ☐ W.11-12.1.C No evidence: ☐	☐ Uses words and phrases that are not appropriate for the audience and purpose	☐ Inconsistently uses words and phrases that are appropriate for the audience and purpose	☐ Consistently uses words and phrases that are appropriate for the audience and purpose	☐ Uses precise language, specific vocabulary, suitable tone, and other techniques to manage the complexity of the topic
Conventions CCSS.ELA-Literacy Standards: ☐ W.11-12.2.E No evidence: ☐	☐ Conventions used interfere with the audience's understanding	☐ Conventions used intermittently interfere with the audience's understanding	☐ Conventions used do not interfere with the audience's understanding	☐ Conventions used contribute to clarity

Compared with numerical scores, which may be interpreted as final judgments and short-circuit useful feedback, labels provide a more nuanced and growth-oriented approach to assessment (Kuepper-Tetzel & Gardner, 2021). Qualitative descriptors emphasize the learning process and signal to students that their skills are evolving rather than fixed. They encourage students to view their current performance as a step on their learning journey rather than a final judgment, which promotes a growth mindset. Descriptive labels also offer clearer guidance on areas for growth and reduce students' tendency to focus solely on point values, shifting their attention to the qualitative aspects of their work and the specific ways they can improve it.

Streamlining the Process

Creating rubrics can be time-consuming, but there are ways to streamline the process and improve efficiency:

- **Use existing rubrics as starting points** and modify them for specific assignments as needed.
- **Limit rubrics to a single page**, focusing on the most essential criteria.
- **Create scalable and reusable rubric templates** that can be adapted for multiple assignments.
- **Use digital tools** such as Rubistar or AI writing assistants to create initial drafts, being sure to review and refine the results for quality and accuracy.
- **Focus on key learning outcomes** rather than trying to assess every aspect of an assignment.
- **Regularly review and update rubrics** based on student performance, feedback, changing student needs, and curriculum updates to ensure they remain relevant and effective.
- **Collaborate with colleagues** to develop shared rubrics for common assignments or skills.

Dovetailing with these last points, middle school teacher Kim Haber explains how her team of three teachers collaboratively refines rubrics through an iterative process. One teacher creates an initial draft, which the team then reviews together, comparing it to the relevant standards. "We need to go over our rubrics at the very beginning of the unit so that we're sure they're right and we're not just improving things at the end."

Even with these efficiency strategies in mind, rubrics initially take a significant time investment, but this upfront effort can lead to substantial time savings down the road. Teacher Brennan Brockbank highlights the efficiency of rubric-based assessment. He says, "It took a lot longer to grade the assessments that were points-based because we were marking a point off here or two points off there." Well-designed rubrics streamline assessment and feedback by allowing teachers to quickly and consistently evaluate student work. Reducing the need to provide extensive written feedback allows teachers to personalize key comments. Effective rubrics also minimize evaluation and grading disputes by making assessment criteria explicit.

Rubrics can also be reused across multiple terms, eliminating the need to re-create assessment criteria for each new class. For courses with multiple instructors, rubrics help ensure grading consistency and minimize time spent on calibration discussions. The investment in creating clear, comprehensive rubrics pays dividends by helping teachers streamline assessment, provide more consistent and detailed feedback, and maintain quality in their assessment tools.

A Focus for Instruction

Identifying essential skills and creating explicit rubrics enables teachers to significantly enhance the clarity and focus of their instruction. Drawing on the key learning outcomes identified, educators can design lessons that directly target critical competencies. Effective rubrics specify clear criteria for evaluating student work in relation to established standards or learning outcomes. They also make instructional goals more transparent and serve as concrete reference points for both teaching and assessment (Arter & McTighe, 2001). Such clarity allows teachers to align their curriculum and instructional strategies more precisely with desired learning outcomes. The combination of identified essential skills and well-crafted rubrics creates a focused learning environment where both teachers and students have a shared understanding of educational objectives, leading to more effective instruction and improved outcomes for students.

Targeted Teaching

Let's say that you want to improve your students' verbal presentation skills. You've designed a rubric with clear criteria for what constitutes effective communication at different levels of proficiency. How can you use the rubric to drive your instruction? First, share the rubric and learning goal with your students. You might start with a hook to capture student engagement—maybe show them a clip from "Talks by Brilliant Kids and Teens," a playlist of TED Talks (www.ted.com/playlists/129/ted_under_20; TED, 2012), and ask them to identify effective presentation tactics they observed. Then compare their observations to the components of effective communication outlined in the rubric. Follow-on practice activities could focus on specific aspects of communication such as clarity of speech, organization of ideas, and engagement with the audience, and your closure activity could be students giving short presentations using the rubric as a guide for self-assessment and peer feedback.

A targeted approach like this helps students understand exactly what they need to improve and provides a clear path for skill development. The rubric also guides you and student peers in providing specific, constructive feedback aligned with essential communication skills and standards. Ultimately, you could assign a culminating presentation, applying the same rubric in a summative assessment.

Middle school social studies teacher Emily Longnecker and her team have developed a comprehensive approach to using rubrics in their classrooms. They create rubrics for nearly all activities, including ungraded ones, to maintain a focus on learning goals. This practice also helps students understand the components of effective academic work. Figure 3.3 is an example of a rubric focused on key elements (i.e., claim, evidence, reasoning) with embedded examples for each performance level.

Providing this level of detail, along with examples, helps students understand both what is expected of them and how to improve their performance. The support afforded by effective rubrics is crucial in fostering student growth. Students can easily identify areas where they need to focus their efforts and understand the steps they need to take to enhance their skills. Rubrics are more than assessment tools; used correctly, they are valuable instruments for learning and self-improvement.

A Shared Framework for Learning

Rubrics are powerful tools for teachers, too. By clearly articulating the components of successful work, they help teaching teams align instruction more precisely with the specific skills and knowledge required for mastery. Students know what each lesson should enable them to know and to do—and, by the end of the lesson, whether they hit the target.

Although rubrics and lesson targets provide a shared framework for learning objectives, they do not prescribe a scripted curriculum or uniform teaching methods. Teachers retain the flexibility to adapt their instructional approaches to meet the diverse needs of their students while working toward common goals. Flexibility is particularly crucial for traditionally underserved students, who may benefit from culturally responsive and differentiated instruction.

Lessons that focus on rote skills and procedures can lead to disengagement and lower academic achievement (Darling-Hammond, 2001). By using rubrics that emphasize reasoning, problem solving, and higher-order thinking skills, teachers can ensure all students, regardless of their background, are held to high standards and are given opportunities for rigorous learning. These opportunities include culturally relevant curriculum and instruction, creating more equitable education for all students. Additionally, well-designed rubrics can serve as scaffolds for assessment for learning—using formative assessment to improve students' performance—promoting student self-regulation and metacognition, which are particularly beneficial for students who may have had limited access to such learning strategies in the past.

Rubrics to Grades

So how do you convert the qualitative assessments produced by the use of rubrics throughout the learning process into quantitative scores for grading purposes? Depending on your learning management system, scores can either be reflected directly in progress reporting or—in traditional, more limited grade reporting platforms—averaged across different criteria or assignments. It is important that final scores for student work follow opportunities to learn, receive feedback, and revise or retake assessments to ensure that students' final grades reflect their best performance and growth over time.

One grading method is to assign numerical values to each performance level on a 1- to 4-point scale (e.g., Emerging = 1, Exemplary = 4). Marzano's (2010) proficiency conversion scale is a research-based approach to translating rubric scores into traditional letter grades. In simple terms, 3.5–4.0 = A, 3.0–3.49 = B,

FIGURE 3.3
Example of History Rubric

Criteria	Beginning	Developing	Proficient
Claim: A direct answer to the question, which restates the prompt for clarity	The claim is unclear, off topic, or does not address the prompt. *Example:* The first humans emerged in central Africa over 250,000 years ago.	The claim is understandable but does not address the whole prompt. *Example*: Who can say when history begins? I certainly am not qualified to answer.	The claim is clearly worded and answers the prompt. *Example:* History begins with humanity's first written records.
Evidence: A summary or quote from a primary or secondary source that directly supports the claim	The evidence seems to have no connection to the claim and may be primarily based on opinion. *Example:* While there are plenty of fossils that support the idea that *Homo sapiens* developed 250,000 years ago, some people think it may have been a lot more recently.	The evidence is on topic but does not seem to directly defend the claim and may not be appropriately cited. *Example:* Herodotus collected stories from around the Mediterranean in a book called *The Histories*. Many historians think this is the first history ever written.	The evidence is appropriately cited, on the same topic as the claim, and clearly supports the claim. *Example:* According to *Ancient World History*, the Sumerians created the first system of writing in 3300 BCE. They used this writing to create the first records of government and business.

Criteria	Beginning	Developing	Proficient
Reasoning: An explanation of the evidence and an expansion of its ideas that demonstrates a clear link between the claim and evidence	The evidence is left without explanation; the piece simply restates the evidence. *Example:* There are lots of people who think that humans may have been aliens from another planet—maybe Mars?	The reasoning may expand on and explain the evidence, but it does not improve the reader's understanding of the claim. *Example:* Despite his reputation as the father of history, Herodotus collected fanciful accounts of giant ants and other myths. Clearly, history had a long way to go.	The evidence is explained in the writer's own words, with reasoning that improves the reader's understanding of the claim. *Example:* Without written records, one generation could not accurately pass their ideas on to later peoples. The Sumerians created the first history when they recorded their daily events, giving us a window into their world.

2.5–2.99 = C, 2.0–2.49 = D, and below 2.0 = F. These parameters or others can be set as defaults in gradebook programs using a 1–4 or 0–4 rubric-based assessment system. The pitfall to avoid is to allow an automated system pegged on 100 percent to convert a rubric score of 3 to 75 percent, which normally would be a C. A 3 on a 1 to 4-point system is considered a demonstration of proficiency or meeting standard. You can also reflect the varying importance of different rubric criteria by using a weighted average approach to give more important criteria a greater influence on the final grade.

Converting rubric scores to letter grades for grade reporting allows schools to meet institutional or systemic requirements for traditional grading formats.

This strategy bridges the gap between the rich, formative feedback provided by rubrics and the summative nature of end-of-term grades and preserves the detailed assessment information gathered through rubrics while translating it into a format familiar to students, parents, and administrators. The method maintains consistency and fairness in grading, as the conversion is based on clearly defined criteria and performance levels rather than subjective judgment and a student's random collection of points on a 100-point scale. Ultimately, such an approach allows educators to leverage the pedagogical benefits of rubrics while still operating within conventional grading systems. (See Chapter 6 for further descriptions and discussion of weighted averages and improved reporting interfaces.)

Spotlight: Embedding Rubrics Across the Classroom Experience

Katie Linklater, Science, Rose Hill Middle School
Redmond, Washington

When Katie Linklater was introduced to rubrics during her teacher training program, she assumed their use was a standard practice in schools. However, upon taking her first middle school job, she discovered that rubrics were outside the comfort zone of many of her new colleagues. "They were using points, and I was talking about standards-based grading," she says. "Those are totally different things."

Incongruity between what teacher candidates learn as best pedagogy and what they experience on the job as novice instructors is not unusual. As Katie continued to advocate with her science teaching team for the use of rubrics for practice assignments as well as other assessments, the school leadership team was prioritizing creation and use of rubrics as a school initiative. Over the next few years, the school transitioned to rubric use across the board.

This transition required subject-area teams to shift to backward design in support of a more consistent approach to assessment. Instead of teaching a unit and then writing a test, teachers now began by examining the standards to develop corresponding rubrics and focused instruction, followed by creating prompts and assessment tasks aligned to the standards. Working together as a team ensures consistency across teaching, assessment, and standards. In a somewhat novel approach, Katie embedded rubric performance criteria directly into student assessments, allowing students to see the target and rating for each test section to encourage self-assessment during the test (see Figure 3.4).

Embedding rubric items in assessments resolves a common issue in which students have difficulty connecting specific questions to the corresponding rubric criteria. Integrating rubric criteria helps students easily identify which tasks relate to each rubric element. After an exam, students can more easily pinpoint areas of strength and those needing improvement, facilitating, for example, more focused preparation for any potential reassessments.

Katie has extended the rubric concept to her classroom management. She created colored posters around the classroom with descriptors as visual anchors of various aspects of their classroom norms (e.g., getting quiet when prompted, arriving on time). Katie tracks class performance using magnets on a whiteboard calendar, fostering a sense of unity and achievement among students without singling anyone out. Class performance on behavior ratings does not affect individual academic grades, which maintains the integrity of academic assessment and provides clarity and consistency.

Because Katie consistently uses rubric terminology for classroom behavior and social norms, students who become familiar with the rating can more easily apply it to their academic work. Using consistent terminology creates a cohesive framework for understanding expectations and performance across all aspects of the classroom experience.

Katie's use of behavior rubrics also aligns with trauma-informed practices, providing structure for her 6th graders as they navigate the complexities of middle school life. Katie recognizes the benefits of providing clear expectations and feedback for students adjusting to the new social and academic environment of middle school, creating a more supportive and predictable learning environment for all students.

Spotlight Questions

- Katie encountered some differences between what she had learned in her preparation program and what she encountered on the job. Have you experienced such contrasts between, perhaps, ideas from professional development you have attended and "on-the-ground" practices at your school? How have you dealt with those discrepancies?

FIGURE 3.4
Sample Test with Embedded Rubric

Ecosystems Model Final Test	Organisms
Add to the food web model of our ecosystem below using the listed organisms. • Draw more circles and label them with the names of organisms. • Draw arrows [→] to show how matter and energy flow. *[Diagram showing circles labeled: Pacific madrone, Caterpillar, Red alder, Salal, with an arrow from Salal to Caterpillar]*	**Caterpillar** eats red alder **Bee** eats nectar from salal, huckleberry, and Pacific madrone **Garter snake** eats caterpillars **Woodpecker** eats caterpillars, Pacific madrone, and salal **Coyote** eats snakes **Black bear** eats evergreen huckleberry **Spotted owl** eats snakes

Developing standard (Level 1)	Approaching standard (Level 2)	Meeting standard (Level 3)	Exceeding standard (Level 4)
Accurately shows who eats whom using one or two of the listed organisms.	Accurately shows who eats whom using some or most of the organisms listed.	Accurately shows the flow of matter and energy with arrows indicating producers and consumers.	Accurately shows the flow of matter and energy with arrows indicating producers, consumers, and decomposers.

- What's one of your takeaways from the example of embedding rubric criteria into an assessment task? What, if anything, might you consider trying with your students?
- Katie found the use of rubrics as anchor charts to support classroom norms to be useful for her students. What kinds of visuals related to classroom norms or academics do you have in your classroom? What refinements or additions might you consider?
- What's one thing from this section that would be interesting to discuss with your colleagues? Why is that?

Benefits of Systematic, Schoolwide Implementation

Physics teacher Brennan Brockbank notes that some teachers in his department used rubrics for grading while others held onto traditional points systems, and the discrepancies were apparent. "A few teachers insisted on each question being worth an arbitrary number of points," he says. "Some were two points, some were five, some were one. The teachers who used traditional grading had a much higher number of students who were not passing. One teacher had double the number of Black students failing than those of us who used rubrics."

Systematic implementation of essential standards and rubrics across a school can lead to significant improvements in both teacher confidence and student learning outcomes. These gains can be observed and tracked at various levels, from individual classrooms to schoolwide data (Panadero et al., 2023). The positive impact extends beyond immediate academic performance, potentially influencing graduation rates, postsecondary education pursuits, and performance on high-stakes tests. Using rubrics particularly holds promise for traditionally marginalized students, with research indicating that clear learning targets and well-designed rubrics can help reduce achievement gaps and promote equity in education (Brookhart & Chen, 2015).

After Katherine Holden's school implemented schoolwide enduring standards and rubrics, they saw a strong correlation between students' performance on their proficiency rubrics and standardized test scores. The correlation of data not only reinforced the value of teacher expertise in curriculum design but also demonstrated the potential of well-implemented essential standards and rubrics to align classroom instruction with broader educational goals and assessments. As Katherine notes, "The clarity and explicitness of these rubrics have made our teaching more focused and effective."

Collaborating with Students

Assessment and evaluation should be collaborative processes involving both teachers and students, rather than actions imposed by teachers on students. Involving students in the use of rubrics is a crucial enhancement of the learning process and promotes student engagement. When students participate in creating, understanding, or refining rubrics, they gain deeper insights into assignment expectations and sharpen their critical thinking skills. Active involvement helps students become self-directed learners, as they better understand the criteria for success and can more effectively self-assess their work (Kilgour et al., 2020).

Discussing rubric criteria and examining examples of varying quality help students develop evaluative skills and become more invested in their own learning outcomes. Additionally, students' involvement with rubrics can lead to increased confidence in their ability to learn and encourage them to set higher goals for themselves. A collaborative approach to assessment also fosters a more equitable learning environment by making expectations transparent and accessible to all students, a practice that "lifts the veil" on how to succeed (Feldman, 2024b). Ultimately, involving students with rubric development and implementation not only clarifies academic standards but also empowers learners to take an active role in their education journey, promoting self-reflection and lifelong learning skills.

Pitfalls of Teacher-Centric Recordkeeping

Tracking student progress is a crucial aspect of teaching, but traditional grading methods often fall short in accurately reflecting student learning and growth. Many teachers organize their gradebooks into categories such as quizzes, homework, tests, and projects. Although this categorization seems logical, it can lead to problematic outcomes when all work is subsequently combined into a single grade, as is common in traditional grading systems. This approach has several drawbacks:

- It disconnects grades from actual learning and growth.
- It conflates behaviors like completing homework with understanding content.
- It establishes the teacher as the sole keeper of grading knowledge, depriving students of valuable learning opportunities.
- It hinders student engagement and self-reflection.

Let's look at some more problematic consequences of commonly used tracking methods that are primarily driven by teachers rather than students.

Overreliance on Summative Assessments

Whereas formative assessment is used to inform instructional steps on each student's journey to mastery, summative assessments are meant to be final evaluations of that learning. Unfortunately, summative assessments such as end-of-unit tests or final exams put a lid on the learning process, missing opportunities for ongoing feedback and adjustment. When teachers rely heavily on this type of assessment to characterize students' performance, it can lead to a teach–test–move on cycle, where students who struggle don't get timely interventions.

Unintentional Bias

Unintentional biases may favor some students while disadvantaging other students; often, these biases are felt by students who are multilingual learners, receive special education services, or come from traditionally marginalized communities. Teacher expectations can be influenced by a student's race, ethnicity, or disability status, which can lead to misidentification of learning needs or inappropriate identification for special education services (Alvarez, 2024).

Lack of Transparency

Teacher-centric tracking processes leave students out of the assessment process, which means they miss out on developing crucial metacognitive skills. Involving students in self-assessment and reflection helps them understand their learning progress and take ownership of their education. In traditional points-based systems, where assignments are given numerical scores without clear criteria and grading lacks transparency, neither students nor other stakeholders are easily able to comprehend what students know and what they still need to learn. Students and their families have difficulty understanding specific areas of strength or needed improvement (Great Schools Partnership, n.d.).

Benefits of Student-Centered Evaluation Practices

Effective monitoring of student progress is crucial, but simply aggregating scores from various assignments into a single grade fails to accurately represent students' growth toward meeting essential learning standards. For progress tracking to be a powerful tool in the learning process, students must be active participants. Involving students in monitoring their own progress transforms tracking from a mere administrative task into a dynamic, student-centered learning experience:

- Students gain more when they understand what they are expected to learn, know where they are in the learning process, and have concrete steps in place to make improvement.
- Student motivation increases when students are actively engaged in the process of learning.
- Teachers save time grading and can use that time to design engaging curriculum or provide feedback to students.
- Students develop self-regulation and metacognition skills as they think about their own work and those of their peers.

Self-assessment is a high-leverage learning strategy that demands significant cognitive effort from students (Frey et al., 2018). Effective self-assessment involves several critical steps. First, students reference a rubric to understand their learning objectives. Next, they gauge their current progress against these targets through self-reflection and analysis. This analysis helps them identify gaps between their current performance and intended outcomes, which supports developing and implementing plans to meet the learning targets. This process not only contributes to rigorous learning experiences and promotes equitable opportunities for all students (Hammond, 2018; Rebora, 2022) but also increases engagement and motivation (McMillan & Hearn, 2008).

Integrating rubrics into assignments ensures students have the tools they need to accurately evaluate their own performance. In art teacher Isaiah Wyckoff's class, for example, students "need to make a claim for their score, and that claim is based on reasoning and evidence; then they add commentary on those things." Isaiah's students become adept at self-assessment and peer-assessment by having the rubric readily available to evaluate their work. As one student noted, "Even if you don't know every word of it, you have it in the back of your head, knowing what the targets are, so you can give good feedback to your friend. It's not just, 'Oh, yeah, it looks fine.'"

Teachers often find themselves overwhelmed with grading, dedicating substantial time each week to the practice. However, by empowering students with self-assessment responsibilities, educators can reclaim valuable time for individualized instruction, lesson planning, and collaboration with professional learning communities.

Teaching self-assessment practices to students also addresses the growing concern for developing "soft skills" and the habits of mind crucial for future academic and professional success. Providing structured opportunities for goal setting helps students cultivate time management, critical thinking, and problem-solving abilities while also boosting their self-confidence. The sense of accomplishment that comes from setting, working toward, and achieving goals is a powerful motivator that students deserve to experience.

Teachers can integrate rich self-assessment opportunities into their classroom routines to actively engage students in their learning process, deepening their understanding and involvement (McTighe & Tucker, 2022). Clear, student-friendly rubrics encourage students to reflect on their work, asking themselves questions like "How can I move today's assignment from the Proficient level to Exceeds Expectations?" Using an iterative process of personal work and revision grounded in a rubric fosters a culture of continuous improvement and self-directed learning.

Student Reflection and Goal Setting

Rubrics provide a foundation for teaching self-assessment and allow students to accurately gauge their performance against proficiency standards. However, to be able to do so, students must understand the progression between each level. Breaking down rubric criteria into concrete, actionable steps helps students accurately assess and improve their skills. This approach not only clarifies expectations but also equips students with the tools to critically evaluate and enhance their own work.

For example, let's look at the analytic writing rubric from Figure 3.2 (pp. 60–61), focusing on the Proficient level for the Organization criterion. Following are several strategies you might use to help students refine their work to meet the specified standards:

- **Analyze exemplar texts** to identify and discuss effective openings, body paragraphs, and conclusions. Include examples with clear and logical structures as well as texts that lack them, guiding students to understand why certain pieces are successful. Model the writing process, verbalizing decisions about organization and transitions.
- **Guide students in creating outlines** that demonstrate a logical progression of ideas. Teach them to break their topics down into smaller, manageable elements and find supporting evidence for each.
- **Provide targeted feedback on student drafts**, highlighting areas where clarity and logic can be improved. Engage students in peer review sessions focused on evaluating the structure and flow of one another's writing, using the rubric as a guide, and demonstrate how to integrate feedback into revisions.
- **Have students practice revising their own work** based on feedback received, focusing on improving structure and coherence. Encourage them to reflect on the feedback process and apply insights to their own writing, fostering a deeper understanding of clear and logical structure.

Once students have completed the instruction–practice–feedback cycle, they are more likely to understand how to use the rubric to succeed with the task; what might have first appeared as vague is now part of their skill set.

This approach to enhance student understanding and performance is applicable across grade levels and content. Mathematics teacher Sara Daley observed significant improvements in student growth when she made learning targets and success criteria explicit: "They could see that they were really good at multiplying fractions because they had high rubric scores. But they could also see where they were struggling." This clarity gave students a sense of ownership over their learning journey. With a visual representation of their progress through rubric ratings, students could easily identify their strengths and areas for improvement. Rather than being discouraged by perceived large gaps in their understanding, students could see their precise standing in relation to the learning target and determine what to do next. Students who have a clear view of their progress are encouraged to persist in their efforts, even when faced with challenging material.

Student-Led Progress Tracking

Turning the responsibility for progress tracking over to students not only lightens teacher workload but also engages students in active reflection on their learning journey. Sara Daley provides her students with a tracking sheet to record their progress in each area (see Figure 3.5) that links their assessments to mathematics standards. When students receive their assessed work, they update their proficiency tracker, resulting in a clear visual representation of their progress toward learning goals. To support the development of organizational skills, have students keep their trackers and assessments in hard-copy or digital folders until the end of the unit.

Student trackers such as the one in Figure 3.5 are versatile tools that can be used in various ways, from formative assessment (helping students identify areas where they need more practice, gauging readiness for summative assessments) through comprehensive assessment tracking (combining formative and summative assessment data, providing a holistic view of student progress and performance}. Student trackers can also be used to guide student–teacher conferences and inform decisions about additional instruction or support. They may help students recognize when they need to seek additional help and facilitate the teacher's ability to provide data-driven guidance for targeted support.

In addition to proficiency trackers, Sara's students complete test tracking sheets after assessments (see Figure 3.6), recording their scores for each section and deciding if they need to retake the assessment (see Chapter 4). Sara offers students flexible retesting options, allowing them to focus on specific areas of improvement rather than retaking the entire assessment. Students articulate their plan for improving their scores, which emphasizes the importance of targeted preparation. The process encourages students to reflect on their learning gaps and develop strategies to address them. By requiring students to outline their preparation plans, Sara reinforces the idea that improved performance typically requires additional practice and study. This process supports academic growth and helps students become more self-directed learners,

FIGURE 3.5
Sample Student Proficiency Tracker

Proficiency Tracker
Learning target: Operations with fractions
Student: Keisha

Standard 6.NS.1A: I can add and subtract fractions.

Date	Assessment	Proficiency Level
10/15	Operations worksheet	2
11/7	Fraction tiles	3
11/12	Operations test	4

Standard 6.NS.1B: I can multiply fractions.

Date	Assessment	Proficiency Level
10/17	Textbook p. 41, problems 6–11	2
10/23	Textbook p. 34, problems 21–29	4
11/5	Process explanations	3

Standard 6.NS.1C: I can divide fractions.

Date	Assessment	Proficiency Level
10/25	Worksheet 4.2	3
10/31	Fraction tiles	2
11/7	Target tables	4

FIGURE 3.6
Sample Test Tracking Sheet

Test Tracking Sheet for _____	
Retest options:	
Score per section (*circle one*)	
Adding fractions	1 2 3 4
Subtracting fractions	1 2 3 4
Multiplying fractions	1 2 3 4
Dividing fractions	1 2 3 4

Are you retesting?   Yes   No
Do you want to keep your test to study from?   Yes   No
In which section(s) are you retesting?   • Adding fractions
                                                                         • Subtracting fractions
                                                                         • Multiplying fractions
                                                                         • Dividing fractions	

Preparation I did for this test:	
If I am retesting, preparation I will do before my retake:	

empowering them to take ownership of their progress while providing teachers with valuable data to inform instruction and support.

Summative Assessment Data and Grades

Ultimately, teachers will need to submit grade reports or, in standards-based grading schools, reports on progress toward meeting standards. Student trackers support end-of-term reporting by helping teachers analyze patterns in performance across multiple assessments. When determining final grades, rather than averaging all rubric scores equally, give more weight to more recent assessments to reflect students' current level of mastery (Guskey, 2015). Look for positive trends in student performance, even if full proficiency hasn't been reached in all the essential standards. Focusing on positive trends allows for recognition of growth and progress. Finally, share tracker data with students and parents to provide a clear picture of growth and areas for improvement, fostering transparency in the grading process. By leveraging student trackers in this way, teachers can formulate grades that accurately reflect students' most recent performances and overall growth, providing a fair and comprehensive assessment for end-of-term reporting.

Engaging Families in the Process

As we have pointed out, traditional letter grades fail to provide detailed information about a student's specific strengths and areas for improvement. By contrast, rubrics break performance down into multiple criteria, each with its own set of descriptors. Even though this system provides more detailed information on student performance, the shift to new grading practices can be challenging for adults accustomed to interpreting a single letter grade. They may struggle to understand how rubric scores translate to overall performance or how they compare to traditional grading systems. To meet this challenge, educators need to invest time in educating both students and families to help them understand the benefits of the new approach.

The use of different terminology across subjects or grade levels can further complicate understanding. Merging multiple criteria into a single grade can cause confusion, making it difficult for parents to determine which aspects of performance carried more weight in the final assessment (Jung & Guskey, 2010). The transition requires clear communication and education from schools to help families interpret and utilize the more detailed feedback provided by rubrics.

Communicate the Benefits

Communicating the benefits of rubrics is crucial. Explain how these tools enhance student learning by providing clear expectations and consistent feedback. For example, you might demonstrate how a writing rubric helps students understand what makes a strong essay, from thesis development to evidence use. As with students, it's important to use straightforward, accessible language instead of educational jargon (e.g., use terms like *clear main idea* rather than *coherent thesis statement*).

Providing examples of sample rubrics and explaining their application in assessing student work can further clarify the concept. A math teacher could share a problem-solving rubric, showing how it evaluates not just the final answer but also the student's approach and reasoning. To promote understanding of expectations, send rubrics home or post them on the student information system before assignments begin. For example, a physics teacher might share their rubric along with a project outline for a science fair experiment.

Share Assessments as a Basis for Discussion

Sharing completed or graded assessments with attached rubrics highlighting areas of strength and opportunities for improvement shows how a student's work aligns with the criteria for success. Encourage families to use the rubrics for discussions at home about student work and progress. For instance, parents could ask their child to explain which level they think they achieved on a rubric and why.

Incorporating rubrics into parent–teacher conferences can guide discussion about student performance and goals. For example, you might use a yearlong reading comprehension rubric to show a student's progress over time and set future targets, or you might have the student take the lead on discussing the learning goal in a three-way meeting or portfolio conference.

Keep the Conversation Going

Providing ongoing communication through newsletters, emails, or classroom websites about how rubrics are being used keeps families informed and involved. You might highlight a "Rubric of the Month," explaining its purpose and how it's used in class. Such strategies collectively help your school community better understand and support the use of rubrics in students' education, fostering a collaborative approach to student learning and assessment.

These communication practices can be particularly beneficial for families in underrepresented or marginalized communities. These families may have encountered systemic barriers to staying in touch with their children's academic progress. By providing clear explanations of rubrics and their purpose, teachers and schools can make the "hidden curriculum" more transparent, ensuring that assessment criteria are explicit and accessible to all families. Clarity can empower families to better support students' learning and engage more effectively with teachers while also minimizing the tendency to see these kinds of grading reforms as somehow lowering standards. Additionally, understanding rubrics can help families advocate for their children's education needs and participate more fully in the school community. By demystifying the assessment process, schools can foster greater equity and inclusion, ensuring that all families have the information they need to support their children's academic success.

Pause and Reflect

Take a look at the following prompts and select a couple that are relevant to you based on where you and your students are related to the use of rubrics and student progress trackers. Reflect on your own, discuss with colleagues one-on-one, or start a discussion with your team.

- How often do your students' assessment results differ from their expectations? Do your students have effective study and practice strategies to prepare for assessments?
- What criteria would your team or professional learning community use to identify priority standards for your subject area?
- What techniques can you employ to guide students in translating rubrics into language they easily understand?
- What specific student habits do you aim to cultivate, and how could introducing rubrics support their development?
- What methods for involving students in monitoring their own progress do you think would be most effective?

4

Redos and Retakes Done Right

Avoiding Miscues and Missteps

Classrooms with a single-shot assessment system fail to account for students' diverse learning trajectories, and traditional grading methods are often biased against external factors affecting student performance such as socioeconomic disparities, language barriers, and personal challenges. Incorporating assessment retakes and redos into middle and high school grading systems offers a way to address all these issues, providing students with the opportunity to improve both their understanding and their grades. Although this approach challenges the traditional model of education, it supports reiterative learning, which builds what Rick Wormeli (2011) describes as "true competence that stands the test of time" (para. 12).

Allowing retakes and redos also promotes a growth mindset, a concept popularized by Carol Dweck (2006): that intelligence and abilities can be developed through effort and learning from mistakes. Students learn to view challenges as opportunities for growth rather than insurmountable obstacles. Additionally, offering redos and retakes can alleviate anxiety and fear of failure, empowering students to explore new ideas and take academic risks.

Conventionally, teachers have mainly granted retakes or redos to students with "good excuses" for underperformance—but, it turns out that in practice, the beneficiaries of these policies are primarily white and Asian American students, by and large effectively excluding Black and Brown students (Feldman & Reed Marshall, 2020; Hough, 2019). To counteract what may be an unconscious bias, it is important to craft guidelines to ensure cultural awareness, academic integrity, and fairness. Carefully crafted, these opportunities genuinely contribute to learning for all students.

In this chapter, we'll discuss how to formulate effective plans and clear policies for retaking assessments; explain how retakes and redos can enhance educational equity without compromising academic standards, ultimately supporting a more inclusive and supportive learning atmosphere; and provide practical guidance for establishing opportunities for all students to demonstrate their true capabilities and achieve academic success.

Ensuring Retakes Improve Performance

Although it may be easy to set a retake policy in motion, it can be difficult to help students perform better during their second attempt with an assessment. Offering retakes without support for students to deepen their understanding is unproductive. Some students may approach a retake as if it were another round in a video game, thinking that somehow their outcome will magically improve on the second try. What students do between their first and second attempts to relearn concepts or build skills matters. If students attempt a retake without doing anything different, chances are, their results will not change.

Sort Out the Issue

It's important to diagnose why the first assessment didn't produce the desired result. Some students need to correct misconceptions or mistakes. Others need to relearn content. Still others need help formulating a plan—some students don't do well on an assessment not because they aren't able to understand the material but because they lack key skills necessary for adequate preparation. For example, Shuang Yang, a Chinese language teacher, had a student who was very talented in languages but had other issues that got in the way: lack of organization, time management, and motivation. In collaboration with the student, Shuang developed a plan to support those issues that incorporated consistent check-ins on progress. They made a to-do list, a timeline, and a catch-up schedule together. Following the plan helped the student better prepare for subsequent assessments. "It's a little more time that I need to spend with certain students," she says, "but it is necessary—at least until they get on track."

Collaboratively Formulate a New Study Plan

Sometimes, when students come up short on an assessment, it is because their approach to preparation was rather arbitrary. Educators in middle and high school (and even college) often presume that their students already possess solid study habits, only to realize this is not always the case. When asked how they studied for a test, a student might say, "Oh, I looked over the chapter in the cafeteria before 6th period." Many secondary students have not yet learned good study habits. The first step in formulating a new study plan is to help the student identify what went wrong the first time around. An Assessment Retake Application Form such as the one depicted in Figure 4.1 walks students through reviewing feedback, reflecting on their preparation, and focusing on what they need to do to improve their performance. This process helps students develop a fresh approach to preparing for the subsequent assessment.

Alternatively, teachers can engage with students one-on-one or in smaller groups to provide support for skill development. Social studies teacher Joel Compton's school schedules "academies" twice a week, during which teachers can work with students individually or in small groups. After one exam, Joel targeted areas that needed improvement with a number of students:

> I have six students coming in from my world history classes that haven't done very well. There is one whose work I couldn't read. I told him, "You're not capitalizing anything"; we're going to work on the grammar. Another student didn't understand their thesis. So there are different areas I'm going to have students focus on to reset those skill sets—and if I have enough time, they can redo the assessment right there.

This kind of strategic work with students aligns with Zaretta Hammond's (2014) recommendation that teachers become cognitive allies to their students by conducting student consults, building learning partnerships, and transforming students from passive recipients of information to active, independent learners. Such advocacy and support also maximize the chances for students to achieve success on their redo.

Review Practice Work

Effective retake strategies require initial assessments to clearly identify students' strengths and weaknesses. Often, students have missed out on crucial

FIGURE 4.1
Sample Assessment Retake Application Form

Student Name: _____ **Class Period:** ☐ 1 ☐ 2 ☐ 3 ☐ 4 ☐ 5 ☐ 6 **Assessment:** _____
1. Which topics or skills did you do well on?
2. Which did you struggle with?
3. Identify the tasks you are going to do in the next few days to help ensure your success on the retake. *Select all that apply.* • Make a study guide for this exam. • Review notes. • Create a digital presentation on the topic(s). • Do an annotation for readings I need to review. • Create a mind map for key content from the readings or chapter. • Create and review flash cards for key vocabulary or concepts. • Other:
4. How did you prepare for the first assessment?
5. In addition to the activities you have indicated above, what else could you do differently to prepare for the retake?
Acknowledgment: *By submitting this form, I ……………………………… (type first and last name) acknowledge that I will study and prepare myself, and that my performance on the retake will demonstrate my growth, knowledge, and understanding of the topic.*

practice tasks that could have addressed these gaps. Incorporating missed assignments into revised study plans is one way to improve preparation.

To reinforce for students the connection between practice and outcomes and to develop their metacognitive skills, some teachers share with their class anonymized data linking assignment completion to test scores. This allows students to independently recognize the relationship between study habits and performance. Reflecting on their own academic efforts leads to improved study strategies among students. As Shuang Yang notes, "Selecting an exemplary reflection to showcase in class not only motivates other students but also emphasizes the value of such work."

Some teachers require students to complete all missing practice work before they can retake an assessment. Others find this approach too rigid, opting for partial retakes focused on areas of struggle and co-constructing individualized study plans with students. Ultimately, the goal is to create a flexible system that supports all students in demonstrating their true understanding and abilities.

Maintain High Expectations

The process of reflecting on one's performance, designing a new approach to preparation, and redoing a project or retaking a summative exam builds real-life skills of preparedness, responsibility, and accountability—and stands in contrast to letting students off the hook by giving them low scores, not expecting them to learn the material, and just moving on.

A deliberative process represents higher standards for student learning. All students should be held to a high expectation of success—regardless of their initial performance, whether they have parents who insist they improve, whether they have time to come in after school, or whether they benefit from intrinsic motivation. Feldman (2019b) argues that making retakes mandatory sends a clear message to students about the teacher's belief in their potential and commitment to their success. Requiring students who have not yet reached proficiency to complete retakes or redos is a policy worth considering, especially since many teachers observe that those who would benefit most from this opportunity often choose not to use it.

Spotlight: Work Smarter, Not Harder
Alex Doucette, Social Studies, White Bear Lake High School
White Bear Lake, Minnesota

Early on in establishing a retake process for his history and economics students, Alex Doucette knew that he wanted to avoid students gaming the system by simply cramming on factoids and retaking a test three or four times until they passed.

His first step was to eliminate multiple-choice assessments; instead, his assessments are more robust, and retakes measuring the same concepts and skills might take a different form from the initial test. Before and after school, or during a half-hour daily advisory period, he works with students to develop study plans to identify the topics they want to relearn. "They can come whenever they have time to do so. You need to figure out a way to make it work so that students aren't afraid to come see you," Alex says. He tells them, "OK, this is the material you want to go over again; this is what I'd like you to try to do." Once students follow the plan, they meet with him to show that they've done the preparation. This approach prevents students from attempting to replicate their previous responses and encourages genuine learning and improvement. Shifting much of the responsibility for retake preparation to students reduces Alex's workload and promotes students' ownership of their learning—a win-win situation for everyone involved. He adds, "I'm 100 percent summative, so that reduces the grade load tremendously. It allows me to manage all this relearning."

Alex also offers different options for students' redos. One is a conventional written retake that closely resembles the original assessment format. Although the questions may be slightly modified, this alternative maintains a familiar structure for students. Another option is an oral assessment, which can allow many students to better demonstrate what they know compared to the traditional format. In his classes, oral exams take the form of one-on-one conversation:

> I'll go into depth and find the breadth and depth of everything that they know, until they don't know any more. I'll take notes on where I think we're at. I'll ask them how they think they did. They're very honest about it.

We do the whole thing, and I give them a grade on the spot. Boom! I update it in the gradebook right in front of them while they're sitting next to me. It's really motivating.

Will offering an oral retake option work for all teachers? Are they valid indicators of achievement? Alex puts it this way: "I think not everybody's comfortable with them. It was the standard for assessing proficiency while in the military for qualifications for high-risk assignments. I got pretty good at being able to assess people and say, yes, I trust them with my life."

Spotlight Questions

- Identify at least one of the ways Alex's retake process has him (and his students) working smarter, not harder.
- What supports does Alex provide for continued student learning and achievement?
- What's your experience with oral assessments? To what extent might you be able to use this format in your own retake process?
- If your school doesn't currently have advisory time built into its schedule, how could you create opportunities for students to meet with you individually to review their performance, make new study plans, and assess their success?

Streamlining the Process

Providing opportunities for students to redo their work or retake assessments takes time—a commodity teachers might not think they have enough of. Teachers who have found success with the process, however, find that the time they spend pays dividends in the end. Systematically implementing retakes reduces the need for them in the long run as students improve their study and preparation habits over time. The investment of resources (including time) in implementing new, more equitable practices is balanced by efficiencies gained in other areas. Following are some strategies and practices that can help streamline the implementation of your new policy for reassessments or assist you in refining an ongoing one.

Adapting School Schedules

Teachers and students need collaborative time to work through the retake process. Ideally, the school schedule has such time built into the week—like Joel's school's academies and Alex's advisory periods—during which students can prepare for retakes with the teacher or a peer tutor, or they can engage in the retake itself. Designating specific time within the school day for additional support and reassessments ensures that all students have equal access to these opportunities regardless of personal circumstances, such as after-school jobs, family responsibilities, or transportation limitations.

Partnering with Other Teachers

Not every school has allocated time in the school day for students to easily access their teachers outside class, which can make finding time for retakes more challenging. One strategy is to team up with other teachers. At one high school in Portland, Oregon, each math teacher opens their classroom one day a week during lunch. They publish a schedule so students know which teacher is available on which day. The teacher that day manages the retake process, and students who have taken the course previously attend and receive tutoring credits for working with anyone who needs additional instruction. If managing retakes and tutoring in the same space seems too complicated, assign one teacher to retakes and another to tutoring.

Building a bank of retake options for students can take time, which is a challenge when teachers are new to a course. One solution is to collaborate with colleagues in the same department or have professional learning teams share the work. As a group, identify key concepts and skills across the curriculum that frequently challenge students, and use these insights to develop retake assessments tailored to different needs and levels of understanding. Dividing the workload allows teachers to specialize in creating retake options for certain subjects or units and results in a richer, more diverse assessment bank.

Collaboration can be facilitated through regular planning meetings in which educators share insights and test items and compare student performance. Beyond building a bank of retake options, this process promotes greater reliability and validity for assessments, helps teachers calibrate evaluation criteria, and informs instructional decision making. Using digital platforms or shared drives to organize and access the test bank allows for easy updates and modifications based on ongoing assessment data. Collaboration like this between teachers can be "the best, most agreed-upon means by which to continuously improve instruction and student performance" (Schmoker 2006, p. 106).

Retakes During Class

What if your schedule does not allow for out-of-class retake opportunities? What if you don't want to ask students to give up their lunch period? One option, especially accessible within the workshop model of instruction, is to conduct retakes during class time. The workshop model facilitates students working on a range of activities concurrently—and those activities can include practice assignments, enrichment tasks, and retake opportunities. Math teacher Sara Daley designates "target table days" for students to self-select learning targets that they need further practice with and collaborate with peers on related activities. Her students are guided by proficiency sheets that link assessments to learning targets and identify which areas they need further experience with.

During these sessions, students who have already achieved proficiency engage in enrichment activities, and those who feel confident in their readiness to retake assessments do so. This setup also provides Sara with time to offer individual support to students. The workshop model supports students' awareness of their current focus and its relevance to their overall learning progression.

Pinpointing Learning Gaps

Although sometimes students "bomb" an entire assessment, more frequently, assessments reveal both areas of strength and gaps in learning. Identifying the learning gaps post-assessment streamlines retake preparation for students and results in less work for you to grade. The first step is to encourage all students to make corrections to items they missed on an assessment. Learning from their own mistakes allows students to clearly see their learning gaps, which in turn enables them to identify which aspect of the assessment they want to retake.

Sara typically devotes time in class to reviewing each assessment, with students using markers to color-code their misconceptions. Students rework each of the questions they missed to prepare to redo the assignment. Because each question is tied to a particular standard, it is easy for students to know which standard(s) they have yet to master. They don't have to retest on the parts that they have shown they know, only on the target they missed. Alex's approach is to use individual student study plans as a basis for focused retakes. When he meets with students to tailor a plan to their learning gaps, they identify areas for the student to review prior to the retake.

Notice the shift in these examples in the way teachers use their time. Instead of spending time regrading entire assessments, they spend it working with students specifically on the areas where they need improvement.

Time and Number Limits

One way to keep retakes manageable (and prevent an avalanche of work for you at the end of the term) is to set a deadline one week before the conclusion of the grading period (Stenhouse Publishers, 2010). However, even this practice can lead to unforeseen problems. Alex Doucette recalls that before his department revised its policy, a few students would want to retake everything during the last three weeks of the term. "It became wildly stressful for the students and had negative consequences on their emotional and mental health," he says. "Their grades suffered because of it, and parents wondered why they were only doing this now." Establishing a progressive timeframe for each retake opportunity ensures that students don't fall too far behind—and keeps you from being buried under a mountain of work at the end of each term.

Once an effective retake process that incorporates reflection, relearning, and preparation is established, you'll rarely find students needing more time to retake their assessments or having to do it more than once. If students are reflecting on their learning, formulating an approach to home in on gaps and addressing those accordingly, and receiving the support they need, you will not need to set a limit to the number of retake attempts. Another way to ensure that students are indeed ready to do their best on retakes is to follow the lead of a Spanish teacher in the San Francisco area who conducts a "retake prescreening" process, which involves students coming in and responding to a few questions. She verifies that students first understand the material being assessed. "If they cannot respond to the pre-assessment questions," she explains, "I sit down and go over the concept with them. I tell them, 'I want you to look at this and study this.'" She then schedules the retake for the following day.

You might be inclined to set limits on retake eligibility or frequency to maintain control and prevent perceived abuse of the system. However, setting such restrictions contradicts the philosophy of continuous improvement and can be inequitable. Limiting retakes to low-scoring students or to a single assessment per term ignores the potential for all students to improve and undermines the growth mindset principle.

Regardless of what retake policy you implement, it is important to remember that learning can occur at any time. In systems where term grade changes are allowed, teachers may find that revisiting content leads to students demonstrating proficiency in previously challenging areas. In such cases, teachers can consider updating prior term grades to accurately reflect the student's current accomplishments.

Addition by Subtraction

Implementing retake/redo policies takes a time commitment. If you fail to adjust other assessment practices, making retakes available to students can lead to an unsustainable workload for you. Unaddressed demands on teachers' time are a common reason why promising reforms are abandoned.

The first step in balancing your workload is to rethink your grading practices. As we discussed in Chapter 1, uncoupling grading from homework, practice assignments, extra credit, and class participation will enable you to focus on providing meaningful feedback. Many schools have adopted grading policies that de-emphasize scoring formative assessments, reducing the need to scrupulously review and document all student work. Sergio López, a Spanish teacher in Connecticut, explains, "It's not like all of a sudden all students want to retake everything. I actually have less grading because students focus on summative assessments instead of me grading every piece of work they do." Using a streamlined approach doesn't eliminate feedback to students but shifts the emphasis to targeted feedback on key assessments, thereby enhancing student performance and reducing teacher burden.

An Insurance Policy for All Students

Students who engage in the retake process and reflect on their study strategies tend to develop more effective study habits, which in turn prepares them better for subsequent evaluations. Students who perform well on a first attempt can bypass the additional effort required for a retake and instead concentrate on advancing their learning journey.

The availability of retakes serves as a safety net or insurance policy for all students, reducing overall stress and enabling them to perform optimally. Fostering a learning environment that emphasizes growth and normalizes reassessment cultivates a sense of well-being among both students and educators.

Supporting Reluctant Students

Creating opportunities for students to engage in retakes can be approached in multiple ways, each with its own benefits. Sometimes students who need the retake process the most are not motivated to take advantage of it. There are myriad reasons for this, and finding out which ones feed into a student's disinclination helps inform how you respond. It could be that the student does not know how to study for a retake or is daunted by their gaps in learning. By the time students are in middle or high school, many have experienced failure, causing them to stop trying, or they have found themselves in deep holes with their grades from which they feel they cannot recover.

Your first step is to develop good relationships with your students and show them that you care. You may need to build trust and establish rapport. Some students take longer to trust adults, including their teachers, due to past experiences with inconsistent or harmful authority figures, cultural differences, or personal challenges that make forming connections more difficult.

To engage, students need to feel safe and cared for (Hammond, 2014). Regularly checking in with students helps them feel secure enough to take educational risks. Staying connected to reluctant students and offering constant and consistent opportunities and invitations is often necessary to entice students to take advantage of the retake process and further their learning.

Being a Warm Demander

Alternatively, some teachers may choose to make retakes a mandatory part of their classroom policy. When teachers demonstrate genuine care for their students' learning and provide the appropriate support, they set the stage for high expectations tempered with empathy and embody the role of "warm demander," a concept introduced by Judith Kleinfeld in the 1970s. Delpit (2012) describes warm demanders as educators who "expect a great deal of their students, convince them of their own brilliance, and help them reach their potential in a disciplined and structured environment" (p. 71). Providing students with cognitively challenging work—as well as the scaffolds needed to succeed—is key to demonstrating your commitment to them. Braiding together expectations with support is particularly crucial when working with adolescents, who are in a critical phase of brain development and may require structured guidance to trust and learn effectively from their teachers. Having a policy of mandating retakes under certain conditions, rather than making them optional, ensures all students have the opportunity to meet high standards and close any learning gaps.

Both strategies, one emphasizing encouragement and the other stipulating a requirement, depend on strong relationships and aim to help students reach their full potential. Educators are best positioned to determine which approach—or what combination of the two—will work most effectively in their unique classroom contexts. Some may find that blending encouragement with clear expectations provides the right balance, ensuring that every student feels both supported and challenged as they strive to master essential skills and concepts

Collaborating with Colleagues

Divergent grading methods can add stress by confusing students about what it takes to succeed. Often, grades don't necessarily reflect what a student has learned but instead show what qualities teachers value (e.g., timeliness, organization, compliance). A more congruent grading methodology among teachers has historically been elusive, and grading practices are not commonly included in teacher preparation programs. Whether "old school" instructors are weighing the merits of grade averaging versus grading on a curve or progressive teachers are grappling with retake policies and the role of homework in grading, variance prevails.

Some schools and districts have directives stipulating that teachers offer retakes or allocate a certain percentage of the grade to summative assessments. However, such top-down initiatives can lead to unforeseen and negative consequences, particularly if teachers have not had the opportunity to pilot them.

Alex Doucette notes the downsides to such mandated policies: "I think that's largely where we end up experiencing some heartache, with teachers and students trying to figure out what it means and not knowing what they are doing. It's one of the pitfalls that people run into when policy comes before practice."

Educators who independently adopt more equitable grading practices, such as allowing retakes, may find themselves at odds with their colleagues. One teacher we know faced criticism from a fellow educator when their reassessment policy prompted questions from students about the lack of a similar policy in other classes. To mitigate such tensions and move these practices forward, we have several recommendations:

- **Discuss your grading approaches in departmental or professional learning community meetings.** Initiating the conversation will shed light on professional practices and may convince others to change their methods.
- **Partner with a colleague who is also open to revising their grading methods and gather data on your results.** Focusing on students—for example, by tracking the number of students benefiting from the policy, performance improvements, and perceptions of fairness and stress levels—can provide valuable insights.
- **Share information with your colleagues in a positive way.** Seasoned educators might be set in their ways. As one teacher we know says, "Change is hard, not easy. If you've been doing something for 10 years and then all of a sudden someone's presenting you a new idea and saying they have a lot of evidence that this new way is probably the best policy, it takes some humility to say you could have been doing this better all along."

Among educators, conversations around changes in practice can continue for months and may lead to an increasing number experimenting and refining their approaches. Fortunately, teachers are quick to recognize effective strategies, and your colleagues may organically arrive at a kind of consensus. Some teachers will be all in, and others will want to move more slowly. Establish a common understanding and agreement rather than highlighting differences. There are many advantages to greater consistency in grading and assessment practices among teachers across all subjects. Chapter 7 will address some strategies for achieving this alignment.

Engaging Families in the Process

Back-to-school nights and parent–teacher conferences offer opportunities to communicate with families about adjustments in grading practices. A proactive dialogue about how you assess student progress helps prevent misunderstandings. Families who learn about test retakes or changes in homework assessment indirectly might wrongly conclude that expectations are lowered or academic rigor is diminished. Your communication should center on how these changes uphold academic standards by encouraging effective study habits and resilience among students. The overarching aim is to foster a collaborative relationship with parents, families, and caregivers, grounded in clear communication about academic expectations and the objectives behind assessment methods.

Spanish teacher Sergio López doesn't have a lot of direct contact with families; his school channels communication through advisors. When he learned that some parents had the impression that grading standards were being lowered and that his class might not be challenging because of his changes to his instructional approach, he asked his students to take a survey about the level of rigor and challenge in his class. His students were forthcoming. They were being held to high standards, and the systems he'd put in place for them to succeed helped them get there. Sharing such survey results with families—relaying students' own point of view—can be the best antidote against unwarranted misconceptions.

Openly discussing experiences, teaching approaches, and triumphs in engaging all students fosters a palpable sense of community and fairness. This holds true whether you're exchanging insights with your colleagues at school or with students' caregivers and families. Collective understanding is not only meaningful but also enduring.

Pause and Reflect

Take a look at the following prompts and select a couple that are relevant to you based on where you are in the area of redos and retakes. Reflect on your own, discuss with colleagues one-on-one, or start a discussion with your team.

- As you review this chapter, what are some of the things you would like to keep in mind as you build or refine your own retake policy with your students?

- What are some challenges to the successful implementation of a reassessment policy that you foresee in the context of your teaching or teacher leadership? What strategies from this chapter might be most useful to you in meeting these challenges?
- How much time do you spend grading? How might you conserve time to make room to support students to prepare for reassessments?
- What ideas do you have for leveraging a retake/redo process to enable students to take more responsibility for their own learning?
- What can you do to get your colleagues as well as parents and families on the same page regarding the value of retakes?

5

Untimely and Unfinished

Alternatives to Punitive Late-Work Policies

You've meticulously planned an extended assignment for your class: a research report, an in-depth essay, or a comprehensive science experiment with a detailed write-up. You've provided clear instructions, outlined specific requirements, and included a rubric. The due date arrives, and you're met with a mixed bag of results that leaves you feeling frustrated and disappointed.

Several students have excuses for why their work isn't ready. Of the submitted assignments, many appear hastily completed, as if thrown together at the last minute. Others have completely missed the mark and will require extensive feedback. The quality falls far short of what you know your students can produce.

This situation is all too familiar to many educators, prompting feelings of frustration with both students and themselves. What happens if we reframe this challenge as an opportunity for growth? Recognizing that teaching adolescents involves more than just imparting subject knowledge is key to alleviating these frustrations. Just as we teach students how to engage in productive group discussions or simplify equations, we must also help them develop good learning habits, including ones around time management and meeting deadlines.

The issue of managing late or untimely work from students lies at the intersection of fairness, student learning, and practical classroom management. To create an environment that truly reflects student knowledge and supports all learners, educators must carefully consider their approach to students handing in assignments outside established deadlines.

The Pitfalls of Punitive Practices

Teachers respond to late work in a variety of ways, many of which inadvertently undermine student learning and exacerbate inequities. Some educators refuse to accept any late work, feeling that doing so reinforces poor work habits and fails to prepare students for the "real world." However, this perspective often neglects to account for the complex realities of students' lives and the primary goal of education: to foster learning and growth.

Other teachers apply grade deductions to late submissions (e.g., lowering the grade by one letter for each day an assignment is overdue). Although this practice is likely intended to motivate students to complete their work on time, it can instead discourage them from attempting to complete missing work altogether, as any potential "good" grade becomes increasingly unattainable.

When educators interpret "high expectations" to include factors unrelated to the learning objectives (e.g., tardiness in submission) in their grading calculations, even students who demonstrate mastery of the content can receive low grades for reasons that have nothing to do with the learning targets. Traditional late-work policies that focus solely on punctuality rather than content mastery both distract attention from students' true understanding of the subject matter and penalize students for circumstances frequently beyond their control. This in turn can lead students to disengage and have a skewed perception of their academic abilities.

Penalizing late work with grade reductions or zero-tolerance policies precludes teachers from accurately assessing student learning. It can also disproportionately affect certain groups of students. Students from low-income families may have limited access to resources, technology, or quiet study spaces at home, making it challenging to complete assignments on time. Other students may have caregiving duties or part-time jobs to help support their families, leaving less time for schoolwork. Students with learning disabilities, those who require additional processing time, and those with mental health issues may also struggle to meet rigid deadlines. Students still developing their English language skills may need extra time to comprehend and complete assignments. And "excelling" students who are involved in sports, arts, and other school activities can find it difficult to manage their time.

Resolving the Late-Work Quandary

Breanne Johnson, a social studies teacher, struggles with the dilemma of penalizing students for circumstances that may be beyond their control versus indefinitely extending deadlines for everything. "How can I effectively support students in meeting deadlines without resorting to punitive measures?" she asks. She's not alone; many teachers find themselves in a quandary about how to deal with late work. Wormeli (2006) recommends beginning by approaching the situation with curiosity, distinguishing between chronic issues and occasional lapses, and tailoring your response appropriately.

To be sure, although allowing flexibility regarding deadlines can promote equity and support student learning, it also presents several challenges for educators in terms of workload management, end-of-term bottlenecks, and post-assessment submissions. The situation requires a thoughtful, well-designed approach. Without careful planning, the extra effort invested in managing late assignments may not translate into increased student achievement and could potentially reinforce detrimental learning habits.

And yes, deadlines matter. Taking a nonpunitive approach to late work does not mean doing away with deadlines and accountability. As Breanne notes, "No 12-year-old is going to perform well without deadlines or structure. That's just not realistic."

In this chapter, we'll explore successful strategies for developing and managing late-work policies—strategies that help you maintain a commitment to equity and support accurate assessment of your students' learning. We'll discuss how to balance flexibility with accountability, encourage timely assignment submission without resorting to punitive measures, and manage your workload effectively.

Supporting timely submission of assignments is rooted in both respect for students and the desire to transfer ownership of their learning to them. By prioritizing demonstration of learning over adherence to arbitrary deadlines, educators can create a more inclusive and supportive learning environment that accurately assesses student knowledge and skills while promoting student success. Following are three practices that can help create an equitable, supportive approach to late work that is also conducive to student achievement.

Project-Based Learning

As we discussed in Chapter 2, project-based learning (PBL) can help make teachers' workloads more manageable while also contributing to an environment that fosters positive work habits and agency. With support, students develop time management and organizational skills and learn to complete assignments and assessments in a timely manner. In addition, PBL is connected to high levels of student achievement (Chen & Yang, 2019; Ertmer & Simons, 2006; Kingston, 2018; PBLWorks, n.d.).

PBL consists of structured assignments that clearly describe requirements or mandatory elements. A key feature of PBL is student choice. Options for project type, method of demonstration of learning, and/or order of learning are built into the practice. Typically, part of the class's daily schedule will include instruction focused on specific project elements, with other times designated for students to explore samples or experiment with ideas. The fact that students often work individually or in small groups makes it easier for the teacher to monitor student progress and intervene with students who are falling behind.

Another feature of PBL is organizational support—checklists, regular progress monitoring, interim deadlines, and self-assessment tools. Feedback, more so than grading, is crucial in PBL (Vatterott, 2015), and PBL activities incorporate teacher and peer feedback routines. These routines offer the teacher another opportunity to work with students who need support in making sure their work is completed in a timely manner.

Through this structured yet flexible approach, students practice essential time management and organizational skills within a supportive framework. Students learn to balance multiple tasks, meet deadlines, and take responsibility for their work, all while receiving guidance and feedback to ensure they stay on track and produce high-quality results.

Flexible Deadlines

Establishing flexible deadlines for student work not only promotes a supportive and inclusive learning environment but also fosters students' development of crucial life skills: time management, prioritizing tasks, and taking responsibility for their work. One method is to set an "ideal" due date alongside an "extension without consequence" date. This automatically provides all students with an extension option, eliminating the need for individual requests and reducing potential cultural communication barriers. Contrary to concerns that such flexibility might encourage procrastination, research indicates that this approach improves work habits and increases assignment completion rates (Fleishman, 2024; Hills & Peacock, 2022). Giving students flexibility to manage their workload effectively can result in a higher percentage of completed assignments. This approach also helps teachers manage their workload. Spreading submission dates out distributes grading more evenly, with most work still coming in by the ideal deadline and a smaller portion arriving later.

Making deadlines flexible stands in stark contrast to applying punitive late-work policies, which, as we have pointed out, can lead to disengagement and often disproportionately affect students facing challenges outside school. Instead, flexible deadlines create a more equitable system that prioritizes learning and skill development over strict adherence to arbitrary timelines. The practice accommodates students with diverse needs, circumstances, and learning paces, preventing external factors from unfairly affecting their grades. Alleviating the pressure of rigid deadlines allows students to focus on producing high-quality work rather than rushing to meet a completion requirement. It also creates a more supportive classroom environment that better prepares students for the realities of managing deadlines in higher education and the workforce, where flexibility combined with personal responsibility are often key to success.

Check-Ins

To head off time management problems that can crop up for larger or long-term assignments, consider designating check-in dates across the time span of the assignment. This progress-monitoring tool can be an effective approach to managing timeliness and late work in support of student success (Berwick, 2022). Breaking down complex processes into a series of smaller, more manageable tasks facilitates student planning and progress. Students are encouraged to work continuously toward course goals while structuring their time and tasks effectively. Check-ins can prevent work from accumulating and help alleviate the stress associated with a backlog of assignments. Moreover, regular check-ins help students develop the habits of work to meet interim goals, thus building crucial time management skills. In addition, spreading feedback opportunities over the length of the project helps teachers avoid an overwhelming influx of assignments to grade, effectively reducing the end-of-term workload.

Incorporating check-ins shifts the focus from punishment for late work to supportive practices to head it off. Teachers can use check-ins to stay informed about each student's progress, allowing for early intervention when needed and providing opportunities to offer feedback while students are still in the process of learning. If a student consistently misses check-ins, it signals to the teacher that additional support may be necessary. Regular check-ins also enable teachers to identify and correct misunderstandings in real time, preventing compounded errors. Check-ins can be flexibly paced, adjusting to accommodate individual students' needs and circumstances.

Implementing a system of check-ins can create a more supportive environment that focuses on ongoing learning and skill development rather than simply penalizing late work. This is another approach that acknowledges the complexities of students' lives while maintaining accountability and supporting the development of important time management skills.

Features of Supportive Late-Work Policies

Positive late-work policies foster communication and reflection, support student academic achievement, and avoid punitive measures. Policies that accommodate extension requests, work-in-progress submissions, and grace periods all encourage students to reflect on their work habits and time management skills, which can be a powerful tool for personal growth and academic development. Teachers, in turn, benefit from taking time to understand the challenges their students face, both in and out of the classroom. This deeper understanding allows educators to offer targeted support, addressing not just the immediate need but also underlying issues that might be hindering a student's academic progress.

Extension Requests

Allowing students to submit extension requests is a proactive approach to managing late work. Requiring students to either meet an assignment's deadline or submit a written request for an extension compels every student to engage with the due date, whether by turning in the completed work or by formally requesting more time (Gonzalez, n.d.). Moreover, extension requests open up a valuable channel of communication between students and teachers.

Implementing an extension request system creates an environment that prioritizes learning and personal responsibility over rigid adherence to deadlines, once again acknowledging the complexities of students' extracurricular lives while maintaining academic rigor and teaching useful life skills. It transforms potential conflicts over late work into opportunities for mentorship, problem solving, and personal growth.

Work in Progress

When students are unable to fully complete an assignment by its due date, submitting work in progress enables them to showcase their ongoing efforts and receive valuable feedback. A partial submission can serve as a checkpoint, allowing teachers to provide targeted guidance on the work completed thus far. Work-in-progress submission may be part of a policy of flexible deadlines; for example, after initial feedback, the teacher and student can identify a final deadline for the completed work. A fluid timeline gives students the opportunity to incorporate the feedback they've received and finish the assignment to the best of their abilities. A work-in-progress submission policy not only encourages continuous engagement with the material but also fosters a growth mindset by emphasizing the iterative nature of learning.

Grace Periods

Offering a grace period for submitting work is an increasingly popular approach to managing late assignments. Grace periods significantly reduce the workload for teachers by necessitating less time spent managing individual extension requests and evaluating excuses for tardiness. Striking a balance between flexibility and maintaining high academic standards, grace periods both promote student responsibility and reduce administrative burden.

A grace period policy typically allows students to submit work within a short window after the official deadline (usually 24 to 48 hours) without penalty or explanation; the short window encourages timely submission while still providing flexibility. To be successful, grace periods should be limited (e.g., 48 hours rather than one or two weeks), as longer grace periods may actually decrease assignment turn-in rates (Berwick, 2022). Students can take advantage of the grace period without providing a reason or requesting permission, reducing the need for evaluating excuses or tracking individual extension requests. Work submitted during the grace period is graded without penalty, preserving the assignment's full value.

Grace period policies promote student autonomy by empowering learners to manage their time effectively and make informed decisions about when to use the grace period, which fosters a sense of responsibility and helps students develop crucial time management skills. Unlike an extension request, students don't need to offer an explanation, which may benefit students who are uncomfortable asking for special consideration. The grace period also provides a buffer for students to handle minor setbacks or unexpected challenges without the need to petition for a formal extension, allowing for greater flexibility in their academic journey.

It is essential to note that simply announcing a "no penalties" policy for late work, without establishing a supportive framework (like those described in this chapter) and clear expectations for timeliness, is likely to reap unintended consequences and be ineffective. Successful reform of grading practices requires a holistic approach that balances flexibility with structure, accountability with support.

Customizing Support for Students

When teachers notice a pattern of late or missing assignments, they often discover that the issue stems from a lack of understanding rather than a lack of motivation—which may necessitate customized support for the student. Math teacher LaRee Ghassemi recognizes the complex stressors facing her adolescent students: "If a student is telling me that they are taking care of three younger siblings until their parents get home, I understand why they are not getting their work done. We'll work together until I can see that they understand the skill or concept. And I may excuse the assignment that did not get turned in."

An individualized approach requires a laser focus on evaluating a student's learning, acknowledging that how and when they demonstrate that learning may require modification to fit their needs. This is particularly crucial considering the state of adolescent students' mental health. Youth in the United States are experiencing a mental health crisis (CDC, 2024). The complexity of modern teen life, coupled with the pressure of college admissions and the need for high grades to secure merit-based tuition support, places additional stress on students, many of whom also juggle significant responsibilities at home.

Although deadlines are important, they can also be stressful. Teachers who embrace equitable grading practices understand the need for both flexibility and firmness when working with adolescents. At times, deadlines must be firm, but in other instances, allowing students some extra time can support increased learning. Adolescents who feel connected to school are less likely to experience poor mental health (CDC, 2024). Connectedness includes students feeling that their teachers and other school adults care about them and their success.

When teachers rigidly adhere to deadlines without considering students' lived experiences, students may not feel seen or cared for. Conversely, when teachers help students meet deadlines—while still expecting them to do the work to meet standards—students understand that teachers have their best interests in mind. If an assignment is important enough to be given, it warrants supporting a student to complete it. This balance of expectations and support to meet those expectations not only promotes equity but also fosters a sense of connection and care, which is crucial for both academic success and student well-being.

Spotlight: A Standards-Based Approach to Late Work

Tim King, Social Studies, Sherwood High School
Sherwood, Oregon

Tim King's school district began experimenting with standards-based grading over a decade ago, and his experience offers valuable insights into managing late work effectively. In core classes, teachers deliberately align assessments and practice work with designated domain standards, creating a clear connection to learning objectives.

Tim's approach to handling late assignments emphasizes intensive feedback and flexibility along with clear guidelines and timelines: "While I maintain certain policies, I've learned to build in flexibility and exceptions to ensure each student has the opportunity to succeed." His strategy fosters student independence through a gradual release of responsibility, allowing him to identify learning trends and provide targeted support where needed.

Tim's department developed a unified late-work policy permitting students to submit work up until each unit's completion. This policy provides students with some flexibility as they work toward mastery but also establishes clear cutoff points. The department has also instituted biweekly flex periods during which students can work one-on-one with their teachers; a multitiered support system for tracking and intervening in attendance, behavior, and academic issues; and departmentwide availability for student assistance. This integrated support system has proven effective, as Tim reflects, "The work comes in when it is still relevant and still supports their learning toward the target. That is critical for my students and for our workload as teachers."

Using a structured yet flexible integrated support system has proven effective. The school maintains academic rigor while accommodating diverse student needs and facilitating teachers' task management. The success of this method lies in its systematic implementation across the department, ensuring consistency and allowing for individual student circumstances. And focusing assessment on how well students have met their learning objectives, rather than on arbitrary deadlines, promotes both equity and achievement—without penalizing students for things that are unrelated to the mastery of the content.

Spotlight Questions

- Tim strives to foster student independence and self-directed learning within workable timelines. What is one adjustment you can make in your classroom to help your students develop independence?
- The use of a comprehensive support system is one of the keys to fostering student learning. Who can you work with in your school to begin a conversation about developing a more supportive structure for your students?
- Tim's department implemented a consistent policy for late work, a system that supports students but also protects teachers from an onslaught of late assignments. Which of these ideas would be worth discussing with your colleagues?

Maintaining a Focus on Learning

Encouraging timely submission of assignments while maintaining a focus on learning can be achieved through thoughtful assessment design and feedback practices. By reducing overall student workload and emphasizing the importance of each assignment, teachers can create a more engaging and effective learning environment for their students and themselves.

Fewer, More Meaningful Assignments

Reducing the amount of work assigned to students to fewer, more meaningful tasks is one way to center student learning, as opposed to grading timeliness, organization, and other nonacademic skills. This approach increases student engagement, reduces the likelihood of late submissions, allows more time for feedback and revision, and enables teachers to focus on crafting engaging lessons, sourcing enriching materials, and providing individualized student support. Getting more learning out of fewer assignments also aligns with research showing that focusing on the quality of student work is often more beneficial than focusing on quantity in promoting student learning (Challenge Success, 2020). As physics teacher Brennan Brockbank noted, "We have no penalty for late work, and we can accomplish that by reducing how much work we assign . . . and having the work that we do assign be so obviously important."

Use Practice Work on Summative Assessments

Allowing students to reference their practice work when they take summative assessments can be a strong motivator for timely completion of the practice assignments. Being able to apply their efforts in a practical way increases the perceived value of practice work; students see a direct connection between their preparatory efforts and the final assessment. It also encourages students to engage more deeply with the material, knowing that their practice will have a tangible impact on their performance.

Conor O'Brien, a high school social studies teacher, only grades assessments, not practice work. His students maintain a log of the practice work, file the log and the work in a binder, and are allowed to refer to the binder during their tests. Students who diligently complete their practice work are well prepared, and they easily see the link between effort and performance. Susan Christopher's (2007) similar policy for her Spanish classes led to an increase in the number of students completing practice work, demonstrating the effectiveness of this strategy in promoting student engagement and timely assignment submission.

If you plan to allow students to reference their practice work during summative assessments, it is important that the summative assessments evaluate students' higher-order thinking skills. The effectiveness of this strategy hinges on crafting assessments that require critical thinking, application of knowledge, and skill transfer, rather than on merely recalling facts or answering simple, surface-level questions. More complex assessments demand that students engage deeply with the material and demonstrate true conceptual understanding, rather than relying solely on memorization or direct information retrieval, which can be duplicated from their notes.

By focusing on meaningful assignments, providing valuable feedback, and creating clear connections between practice and summative assessments, teachers can foster a learning environment that naturally encourages timely work completion while prioritizing student learning and growth.

Handling Poor-Quality Late Work

Another policy shift to consider is capitalizing on students turning in late submissions of poor quality by recasting a potential setback as a valuable learning experience. Rather than simply assigning a low grade, provide brief, targeted feedback that highlights key areas for improvement, helping students understand their shortcomings but also guiding them toward better performance. A planned response that includes the following components can help students develop strategies to avoid similar late-work issues in the future, promoting better academic performance and personal growth:

- **Reflection:** Students who submit poor-quality late work complete a brief reflection form asking them to identify challenges they faced (e.g., time management, misunderstanding the assignment) and specific areas of their work they feel they need to improve on.
- **One-on-one or small-group support:** The teacher reviews the reflection form and schedules one-on-one or small-group sessions to provide additional guidance on the assignment.

- **Opportunity for resubmission:** After the support session, students are given the chance to revise and resubmit their work. The resubmitted work is graded with an emphasis on demonstrated improvement and mastery of the content, transforming a challenging situation into an opportunity for holistic student development.

Offering only a limited window for revisions can be effective in emphasizing the importance of timely work. Time limits foster a sense of urgency and responsibility, encouraging students to act promptly on feedback. Moreover, these situations present the opportunity to engage students in meaningful discussions about study habits and time management.

Science teacher Tim Larsen's school has a policy that any late or revised work needs to be turned in before the last two weeks of the grading period. Within that policy, each teacher is allowed to apply variations to meet their course goals. Tim allows his students to revise and resubmit before a stipulated date, telling them, "I'll accept it up to a certain point, but if you turn it in late, then you don't have the ability to revise it after I grade it." This motivates students to turn in work on time so they can receive and incorporate Tim's feedback, which in turn allows them an additional chance to show their learning.

Continued Learning and Growth

Summative assessments serve as logical cutoff points for accepting related practice work, as they typically mark the culmination of a learning unit or topic. But what if we viewed summative assessments as checkpoints on the learning journey rather than absolute endpoints? This allows for a more fluid and continuous learning process and communicates to students that learning doesn't stop with a test but continues to evolve and deepen over time. There are ways to balance the need for summative assessment with students' needs for continued learning and growth.

Allow Summative Assessment Retakes

In Chapter 4, we discussed retakes. Implementing a retake or revision policy for summative assessments allows students to demonstrate improved understanding after receiving initial feedback, promoting a growth mindset and encouraging ongoing engagement with the material.

Offer Post-Assessment Assignments

Providing follow-up assignments that build on previously assessed material encourages students to apply their knowledge in new contexts or at higher levels of complexity. For example, many curriculum standards relate to the ability to support a claim. Because students are developing this skill throughout the span of a course, you can provide opportunities for instruction and practice multiple times a year. Subsequent learning opportunities should match student needs, taking into consideration whether students need to revisit the skill or are ready to expand on it.

Alter Prior Grades

In courses where the conceptual framework and abilities in essential skills and standards develop over the course of an academic year, some teachers have had success with policies that allow them to revisit and raise a previous term's grade when students demonstrate proficiency by the end of the succeeding term. This practice reinforces the idea of continuous improvement for students.

This type of recursive grading policy, like those that prioritize the validity of assessments later in the term over earlier evaluations of learning, is rooted in a mastery learning model. Learning is an ongoing process, not a single event, and students' understanding and skills can develop significantly over time, which aligns with the idea that the ultimate goal of education is not just the acquisition of knowledge at a specific point in time but also the development of lasting understanding and capabilities. Mastery learning more accurately reflects a student's final level of achievement in a course, providing a more valid representation of successfully meeting targeted standards.

Standards-Based Grading: A Paradigm Shift

Standards-based grading offers a paradigm shift by transitioning the focus from when students complete their work to whether they meet established learning objectives. This practice allows for a more flexible, student-centered approach to assessment and transforms the way teachers interact with deadlines and manage late work. In standards-based grading, students have multiple opportunities to demonstrate mastery. The most recent evidence of learning is used to assign grades, and academic achievement is separated from work habits or timeliness. The focus on using evidence to assign grades recognizes that learning occurs at different rates for different students and values the end result of learning over the path taken to get there.

However, even within this framework, some time-based structure is beneficial. Setting "soft" deadlines helps pace learning and provides a schedule of crucial feedback opportunities, whereas end-of-unit or end-of-term cutoffs ensure comprehensive curriculum coverage. As art teacher Isaiah Wyckoff sees it, "We need to teach both the academic content and important habits of mind. This includes teaching students the importance of turning things in on time, which is part of building their character." The challenge is how to teach these skills simultaneously.

Isaiah allows students to submit work up to two weeks after the original deadline. If a student hasn't submitted the work within this period, they must develop a different project or assessment based on the same standards, including creating their own rubric. Given that the students at Isaiah's school are already used to working with rubrics, standards, and PBL, a policy that allows them to tailor their project designs and integrate evaluation criteria is seen as a creative opportunity and an extension and synthesis of learning, rather than a punitive consequence.

The Benefits of Constructive Late-Work Policies

Adopting constructive alternatives to punitive late-work policies represents a significant shift in educational practice, one that yields substantial benefits for students. Moving away from rigid, penalty-based systems can create an environment that nurtures a growth mindset and builds resilience in learners. These methodologies allow students to view mistakes as opportunities for improvement, develop crucial time management skills, and focus on mastering content rather than meeting arbitrary deadlines.

The results of implementing such policies are compelling: improved learning outcomes, reduced stress, and a more positive attitude toward education (Hills & Peacock, 2022; Orttel, 2023). Students learn to take ownership of their learning process, developing skills that will serve them well beyond the classroom.

By embracing the alternative strategies we've discussed in this chapter, teachers can create a more equitable, engaging, and effective learning environment that not only addresses the immediate issues related to late work but also equips students with valuable life skills and a healthier relationship with learning. As you continue to evolve your educational practices, these strategies will support your journey toward an equitable, student-centered, growth-oriented approach to assessment and grading.

Pause and Reflect

Take a look at the following prompts and select a couple that are relevant to you based on where you and your students are regarding untimely work. Reflect on your own, discuss with colleagues one-on-one, or start a discussion with your team.

- Which unit in your curriculum would be enhanced by incorporating PBL (short-term or long-term)? What strategies can you implement to help students develop organization and work completion skills throughout the project?
- Which elements of late-work policy can you and your colleagues find common ground on?
- When reviewing your curriculum, which assignments are essential for student learning? Which assignments might be unnecessary or redundant?
- Considering your subject matter, what is a reasonable time frame for students to complete revisions, retakes, and redos? What specific support or resources do your students need to be able to revise and improve their work effectively?

6

Upgrading Your Gradebook

Transitioning to Practices That Reflect Student Learning

There is a growing awareness among educators that traditional grade books and grading policies often distort student learning. Transforming these systems, however, is challenging. The dissonance between equitable assessment practices and outdated grading structures is at the heart of grading reform efforts—and the conflict can reveal deeper cultural beliefs, particularly regarding teacher autonomy. Science teacher Kim Haber, for one, observes that some colleagues saw "their grading practices as their personal domain [because] requests for transparency challenged their established behavioral management strategies." Some teachers, like middle school teacher LaRee Ghassemi, find themselves navigating the transition between traditional and standards-based grading by making compromises to bridge the old and new systems. In LaRee's school, this means implementing rubrics aligned with standards while maintaining a traditional report card format.

Ultimately, traditional gradebooks function as tools of inequity, emphasizing compliance and privilege over authentic learning. In this chapter, we will explore the philosophical dilemmas and practical hurdles of gradebook reform and provide options for navigating technical gradebook limitations and prioritizing equitable assessment. With the tools and strategies we describe, you can transform the contents of your gradebook from what students might view as a cryptic repository of teacher preferences into a clear, equitable reflection of student achievement.

The Pitfalls of Traditional Grading Scales

Traditional gradebooks, structured around weighted categories and percentage scales, misrepresent student learning through systemic biases and mathematical inaccuracies. They often conflate academic mastery with behavioral compliance, embedding racial, gender, disability, and socioeconomic biases into grading practices. As we discussed in Chapter 1, grading subjective categories such as "participation" or "effort" disproportionately penalizes marginalized students, as implicit biases can shape teachers' perceptions of these behaviors. This is a pattern well documented in classrooms taught by white teachers, where Black students often are rated as poorer "classroom citizens" despite equivalent engagement (Downey & Pribesh, 2004).

As mentioned previously, mathematically, the 100-point scale skews toward failure, with 60 percent of its range representing failing scores. Averaging performance over time compounds this inequity; students who master content late in a term see their growth obscured by early struggles. Weighted categories exacerbate the problem by prioritizing arbitrary metrics over demonstrable mastery.

These systems can also weaponize grading as behavioral control through punitive policies such as giving zeros for missing work or imposing penalties for late submissions (see Chapter 5), disproportionately harming students who lack structural support. Current learning management systems (LMS) can further entrench inequities by automating these biases—for example, by converting a rubric score of 3 out of 4 to a 75 percent (a C) even though the 3 is meant to represent proficiency. Such mechanized scoring strips teachers of agency, replacing their professional judgment with rigid algorithms that prioritize efficiency over accuracy, and it may also reflect the biases and limited educational experience of computer programmers, who often lack formal training in pedagogy.

Points-based grading perpetuates a transactional view of learning. Students fixate on accumulating points rather than engaging deeply with content. Teachers may cling to point systems to avoid justifying evaluative decisions or because they simply lack familiarity with better alternatives. The culture of points collection stifles risk taking and intellectual curiosity as grades become commodities to negotiate for rather than feedback for growth. The result is a systemic failure to communicate what students actually know, rendering grades ineffective for both guiding instruction and supporting learners.

The Problem with the 50 Percent Floor

Many teachers embarking on reframing their approach to grading consider the establishment of a 50 percent minimum on the traditional 100-point scale (i.e., no grade is lower than 50 percent, mitigating the mathematical problem of inflating the disproportionate impact of 0-point assignments in an averaged grade) as low-hanging fruit they can target to begin their journey. Incremental changes such as this seem less risky than a wholesale reordering of assessment and gradebook indicators. However, setting the floor at 50 percent fails to address the root causes of grading problems. The 100-point grading scale is inherently problematic, offering an illusion of precision while leading to greater subjectivity and diminished reliability (Guskey, 2013). In addition, minimum-grade policies fail to address problems such as a lack of clearly defined scoring criteria and the need for a limited number of grading categories. As we discussed in Chapter 3, grading scales limited to four to seven levels lead to optimal validity and reliability (Lozano et al., 2008; Preston & Colman, 2000).

The minimum-grade approach is also unlikely to convince those reluctant to change; they may argue that it gives students "something for nothing" (Carifio & Carey, 2009). These teachers believe students who miss an assignment should receive a zero. They contend that the 50 percent floor leads to grade inflation and social promotion, even though empirical evidence does not support these claims. Still, minimum-grade policies "address only symptoms of problems while leaving crucial issues related to consistency and accuracy in grading unresolved" (Guskey et al., 2024, p. 72). If we want to truly transform grading practices, we must move beyond superficial fixes.

Principles of Standards-Based Grading

The path to meaningful change must be built on a solid foundation. Transitioning to standards-based grading requires identifying essential standards, developing robust standards-aligned assessments, creating standards-aligned rubrics, and gaining buy-in from stakeholders (e.g., colleagues, students, families). Planning and clearly communicating the steps toward implementation will help preclude any surprises regarding the content and framework for assessments. A transparent approach also promotes cooperation and consensus, both of which are vital to the sustainability of any grading reform.

With standards-based grading, teachers' gradebooks are organized around specific learning objectives and track student progress toward mastery of standards. This approach shifts the focus from percentages and point accumulation to a clear representation of student learning. Aligning gradebooks to priority standards creates a powerful tool that accurately communicates student growth and achievement, not only enhancing the validity of grading practices but also providing meaningful insight into students' academic progress. To get started, you will need to take the following steps:

1. **Organize by standards.** Replace traditional assignment categories (e.g., homework, tests) with your identified essential standards or learning objectives. Set up your gradebook to allow you to enter rubric scores (e.g., a scale of 1–4) rather than points or percentages.
2. **Weight student work appropriately.** Reflect on the importance of different rubric criteria. If some standards of a rubric are more essential or important than others, consider using a weighted-average approach. Ensure that recent evidence of learning carries more weight than earlier attempts to reflect student growth over time.
3. **Plan for reassessment.** Build in mechanisms to update scores as students demonstrate improved mastery.
4. **Align reporting methods.** Adjust your LMS settings to generate reports that clearly communicate standards-based progress.

The ideal time to implement any changes to grading practices is at the start of a new academic year or semester. A clean break allows for clear communication with students and parents about the new system, alignment with curriculum mapping and pacing plans, and time to adjust and refine practices without disrupting ongoing assessment. Midterm implementation is possible when necessary, using a phased approach, implementing the new system for upcoming units while maintaining previous grading methods for those completed.

What a Standards-Based Gradebook Looks Like

Organizing your gradebook by standards keeps your focus on learning targets and on each student's progress toward achieving them over time. The first table in Figure 6.1 provides an example of a science teacher's gradebook with progress visualization for four summative assessments according to the course's essential standards. This allows you to see individual proficiency trends for each student across the term. Notice that not all essential standards are assessed by each of the four assessments and that not all students' progress on each standard trends toward greater proficiency. For example, it appears that Minh has been making progress on all four standards but "bombed" the fourth assessment. This type of progress monitoring alerts you to times you might need to check in with a student about an uncharacteristic hiccup and perhaps offer a retake or redo (see Chapter 4). The chart also shows that Jacob consistently struggles with the energy and transformation standard, a pattern that suggests a need to identify specific learning barriers, develop a tailored study plan, and provide an opportunity for reassessment.

Digital gradebooks can be set up to offer additional filtered views, such as one in the second table, which is useful for comparing student performances on the same assessment, enabling the teacher to assess the whole class's

FIGURE 6.1
Two Views of a Gradebook Organized by Standards

	Learning Outcomes															
	Scientific Inquiry				Structures and Properties of Matter				Energy and Transformation				Earth Systems			
Maya	2	3	4	4	1	3	n/a	3	n/a	3	4	4	n/a	3	4	3
Alejandro	1	2	3	3	1	2	n/a	3	n/a	2	4	4	n/a	3	3	3
Aaliyah	2	3	4	4	1	3	n/a	4	n/a	2	3	3	n/a	3	4	4
Minh	1	3	4	2	2	3	n/a	1	n/a	3	3	1	n/a	2	4	1
Sofia	2	4	4	4	4	4	n/a	4	n/a	3	4	4	n/a	2	3	4
Jacob	1	2	2	3	2	1	n/a	3	n/a	2	2	2	n/a	4	4	4

(continued)

FIGURE 6.1
Two Views of a Gradebook Organized by Standards (Continued)

		Maya	Alejandro	Aaliyah	Minh	Sofia	Jacob
Assessment #1	Scientific inquiry	2	1	2	1	2	1
	Structures and properties of matter	1	1	1	2	4	2
	Energy and transformation	n/a	n/a	n/a	n/a	n/a	n/a
	Earth systems	n/a	n/a	n/a	n/a	n/a	n/a
Assessment #2	Scientific inquiry	3	2	3	3	4	2
	Structures and properties of matter	3	2	3	3	4	1
	Energy and transformation	3	2	2	3	3	2
	Earth systems	3	3	3	2	2	4
Assessment #3	Scientific inquiry	4	3	4	4	4	2
	Structures and properties of matter	n/a	n/a	n/a	n/a	n/a	n/a
	Energy and transformation	4	4	3	3	4	2
	Earth systems	4	3	4	4	3	4
Assessment #4	Scientific inquiry	4	3	4	2	4	3
	Structures and properties of matter	3	3	4	1	4	3
	Energy and transformation	4	4	3	1	4	2
	Earth systems	3	3	4	1	4	4

strengths and areas for growth. Another view could show student completion of formative work aligned with each summative assessment, facilitating teachers and students to correlate practice work with their assessment results and adjust preparation for reassessments accordingly. Remember that, although digital grading systems are valuable organizational tools, you must maintain an active role in the assessment process, as technology can guide you but not replace your expertise. As science teacher Dan Robinette observes, "Sometimes, teachers want the computerized gradebook to make the hard decisions for them. But the final judgment [of student learning] requires our professional insight and consideration of various factors that technology alone can't fully capture."

It is crucial to recognize that even professional evaluation can be influenced by unconscious biases stemming from cultural differences, personal experiences, or preconceived notions about student abilities. The most effective grading approach combines the efficiency of digital tools with nuanced, bias-aware professional judgment. Regular reflection on grading practices can help maintain more equitable and objective assessments. Some gradebook interfaces offer "blind" or "anonymous" grading functionality, hiding student names and other identifying information. By removing these potential sources of bias, the system helps minimize unconscious prejudices that might influence grading decisions, promoting a more equitable and objective assessment process.

Simplified and Weighted-Average Grading

Grading in the modern era involves a delicate balance between comprehensive assessment and practical limitations. Although the ideal gradebook would allow teachers to track student progress across multiple standards, LMSs may have constraints that necessitate a simplified approach.

In practice, this means teachers often resort to entering a single overall average rubric score for each assessment. Consider a summative assessment evaluated on a 4-point performance indicator rubric. If you assess students on five standard criteria, a student who receives two 2s and three 3s would have a score that averages to 2.6. However, this simplified approach might misrepresent the importance of each criterion. Certain standards (also known as *enduring standards*) may be more crucial to future student success. To address this problem, you could implement a weighted-average grading system.

Social studies teacher Conor O'Brien uses a weighted-average grading system in his sophomore world history class, assigning 60 percent of the grade to skill standards (e.g., logic of argument) and 40 percent to content standards (e.g., outcomes of the French Revolution). His emphasis on skills is deliberate: "My goal is to prepare them for junior year by focusing on developing thinking skills rather than memorizing content." His gradebook automatically calculates the weighted percentages, streamlining the process.

This approach is a way to acknowledge the varying importance of different rubric criteria, ensuring that each aspect of student performance is evaluated according to its relative significance. It allows work toward achieving more critical standards to have a greater influence on students' final grades, aligning assessment more closely with education priorities. However, it's important to be mindful of not overcomplicating grading methods. Your students need to understand why they receive the marks they do. Weighted averages are not as nuanced and comprehensive as standard-by-standard progress reporting, with or without holistic letter-grade conversion.

Some LMSs allow teachers to input rubrics and specify simplified or customized weighted averaging to automatically calculate scores. Some teachers develop conversion scales with grade cutoffs tailored to their own professional judgment, and still others depend on Marzano's conversion scale (see Chapter 3). In these ways, both simplified and weighted average grading can be used with rubrics and standards-based assessment while maintaining consistency with traditional marking systems.

Prioritizing Students' Current Understanding

As student performance improves across multiple criteria and standards, teachers should place greater emphasis on more recent assessments. The fact that students may not have known how to do something previously is irrelevant to what they can do now. There are grading methods that prioritize students' current understanding and abilities, helping teachers move away from traditional points-based systems that average all of a student's scores over time. Prioritizing current understanding and continuous improvement helps provide a more accurate picture of student learning and supports long-term academic growth.

The approaches described here align strongly with the principles of standards-based grading, which focuses on measuring student progress against specific learning objectives. They encourage students to view learning as a continuous process and seek opportunities for improvement throughout the grading period. These approaches also share some common characteristics:

- **Standard-by-standard evaluation.** Each learning standard is evaluated separately, typically using a four-level rubric.
- **Holistic assessment.** The final course grade is determined by looking at the overall pattern of performance across all standards.
- **Emphasis on mastery.** The final grade reflects a student's level of mastery by the end of the grading period, not an average of all attempts.
- **Professional judgment.** Teachers use their professional judgment to determine a final letter grade based on the preponderance of evidence across all standards.

The *most recent grading* method calculates the most recent score achieved on a summative assessment. This approach is especially helpful in courses where students start with little knowledge or skill and improve over time, as it prevents early low scores from disproportionately affecting the final grade. Using the most recent grading method offers several advantages:

- It is easy to understand and explain.
- It provides an accurate representation of the student's current level of mastery.
- It is equitable, ensuring that all students, regardless of their initial pace or struggles, have an equal opportunity to showcase their ultimate growth and mastery of the subject matter.
- It provides teachers with a high degree of control; teachers who feel that a student's most recent score doesn't accurately reflect their abilities can administer a new assessment.
- It is flexible, allowing teachers to quickly respond to student progress, ensuring a more accurate representation of a student's current abilities over time.
- It can be adjusted to accommodate changes in education standards, to ensure consistency across subjects, or to address feedback from teachers, students, and parents when grades don't accurately reflect performance.

Adam Green, a science and math teacher, uses the most recent of three summative assessment scores to reflect student progress for each of his courses' learning targets by the end of the semester. This allows him to focus on students' most current level of understanding and performance. To convert students' scores to the letter grades expected on the school's report card, Adam has developed a "logic rules" chart:

- For an A,
  — Most marks must be Meeting or Excelling.
  — Some marks may be Developing.
  — No marks may be Beginning.
- For a B,
  — Some marks must be Meeting.
  — Most marks must be Developing or higher.
  — One mark may be Beginning.
- For a C,
  — Most marks must be Developing or higher.
  — Some marks may be Beginning.
  — All learning targets must be assessed.
- For a D,
  — Almost all learning targets must be assessed.
  — Some marks must be Developing.
- For an F,
  — There is no evidence for a majority of learning targets.
  — Results don't fit into other categories.

Adam's method for determining holistic grades is easier to explain to students, families, and other stakeholders than complex mathematical calculations or algorithms, providing a clear and understandable way of assessing a student's achievement across a set of aggregate scores. This transparency leads to a better understanding of grading practices and increased trust in the grading system. Adam's grading method and logic rules are explained in his course syllabi, and he reviews them with students and families to make sure there is a common understanding regarding how progress on learning targets will be reflected in final grades.

Sustained progress grading is a method that emphasizes consistent improvement over time. This process considers a student's ability to maintain and build on their understanding of key concepts throughout a grading period. It involves looking at a series of assessments to determine if a student has consistently demonstrated mastery of specific standards or skills.

French teacher Rachel Veto observes, "Toward the end of a term, students often face various challenges that might affect their performance. As a result, their final grade may not always reflect their best work." In her approach to sustained progress grading, students need to demonstrate proficiency (3 on the course rubric) three times throughout the term to earn an overall Proficient rating. This method focuses on personal improvement, showing growth when possible and maintaining an improved level of understanding. The advantages to sustained progress grading include the following, though it may necessitate more frequent assessments, as teachers need to consistently track and document students' ongoing mastery of standards:

- The final grade is more representative of a student's consistent understanding and performance, instead of being overly influenced by end-of-term circumstances.
- Students are relieved of the pressure of hitting the target on every assessment; instead, they learn to prioritize continuous development.
- It provides a more comprehensive view of student growth over time.

The *decaying-average method* gives more weight to recent performance while still considering past achievements. It recognizes that students' knowledge and skills change over time and can provide an accurate representation of their current abilities. In this system, older grades gradually lose their impact on the overall score as new assessments are completed. Typically, the last summative assessment is weighted most heavily (up to 80 percent of the overall grade), and an average of all previous assessments makes up the rest. This method has the following advantages:

- It focuses on measuring student growth and current mastery of specific learning standards.
- It reflects progression by giving more weight to recent performance.
- It encourages continuous improvement and doesn't overly penalize students for early struggles.
- It can motivate students to consistently engage with the material, as each assessment contributes to their final grade, but with an emphasis on demonstrating sustained mastery.

One disadvantage to the decaying-average method is that it can lead to students attempting to game the system, focusing only on the final assessment and neglecting to put forth effort throughout the year. Tim Larsen, a science teacher at one school utilizing the decaying average, observed that many students thought, "This isn't going to matter much in the end. So what's the point of me doing that early stuff?" By contrast, art teacher Isaiah Wyckoff framed the issue as a balance between teaching academic skills and habits of mind.

To address these concerns, their school adjusted the formula, reducing the weight of the final assessment as a way to motivate students to engage more consistently throughout the year. Further refinements led to a hybrid approach: decaying average for concept-based standards and simple averaging for skills-based standards. For example, in science classes, content-related standards such as understanding the periodic table are calculated using the decaying-average method, and skills-based standards such as planning and carrying out investigations are calculated by averaging all assessment scores. This blended approach strikes a balance by placing emphasis on recent performance to evaluate conceptual understanding while ensuring that students are incentivized to work on skills development throughout the course.

Spotlight: A Collaborative Journey
Katie Green, English Language Arts, Highland High School
Bakersfield, California

English teacher Katie Green felt lucky to work within a strong professional learning community. In their initial steps toward grading reform, the team first endeavored to understand what the curriculum standards for their domain truly meant, then decided which ones to prioritize and how to assess them. They identified which standards to focus on for each unit and semester, developed rubrics, created assessments, and built the units. Katie recalls, "It was a process of backward planning, starting with the priority standards in mind. I didn't initially realize how crucial this approach was, but it's been fundamental to our work on equitable grading." Administration support for this work on alignment, coupled with teacher discourse on Joe Feldman's "Grading for Equity" (2019b), catalyzed Katie's transition to reformed grading practices.

Deciding to implement their new grading policy at the beginning of the 2019–20 school year, the teachers were motivated by the interconnected nature of their reforms. "Everything we were working on—pacing, the curriculum—they all followed from our priority standards and agreements on equity and grading practices," Katie explains. Their decision proved to be a catalyst for rapid learning and a step toward transformative change—until it was all abruptly interrupted by the COVID-19 pandemic. For Katie, this period of imposed distance learning brought to the forefront the negative effects of traditional grading systems. "Once you see how implicit biases and flawed systems marginalize some kids and privilege others—across socioeconomic, ethnic, and racial lines, no less—you can't unsee it," she says.

During the pandemic, many school districts focused on establishing minimum grade requirements. Katie's team took a different approach. They concentrated on defining all levels of performance. For example, when debating how to label the level beyond Proficiency, they settled on the label Mastery to represent the top tier of achievement. Katie stresses, "Our definition of mastery is attainable for all students, regardless of how many attempts they need to achieve it. This is crucial because mastery might look different for each student in terms of how it is demonstrated."

To determine grades based on student progress on the standards, Katie and her team use logic rules based on the best or most recent performance. Their nuanced approach to grading balances recency with the teacher's professional judgment regarding validity, depending less on mathematical calculations and more on logical principles. The team has implemented a system that incorporates ongoing assessment of core standards across all summative evaluations, which ensures that students have multiple opportunities to demonstrate mastery of fundamental skills.

Katie and her team's effort to provide a fair and accurate representation of student progress is encumbered by an LMS that is out of sync with standards-based grading. The LMS gradebook defaults to points and percentages, requiring manual configuration each term to align with standards-based grading principles. Katie has developed a workaround, but the far-from-intuitive process deviates significantly from the district's default settings, adding another layer of complexity to the grading process.

The misalignment between progressive grading philosophies and traditional LMS infrastructure is a common challenge in transitioning to standards-based grading. This disconnect creates additional work for teachers who are committed to equitable grading practices and potentially discourages wider adoption of these methods. Katie, like other teachers involved in equity grading reforms, sees this process as an ongoing, iterative change that requires buy-in across the entire campus. She contends that standardizing these grading practices across the school is crucial for the success of this transition, and that ideally any LMS would also be aligned. "Often, the decisions regarding the LMS are based on budget or other considerations, but ideally it'd be better to decide on common agreements around grading before you choose a platform, and then make sure the platform will serve your intentions."

Spotlight Questions

- Much of Katie's move toward grading reform was sparked and abetted by her collaboration with a collegial team. In what ways have you addressed grading reform with a teaching team? What have been the positive results of these interactions? The negatives?
- How does your school's LMS enhance or inhibit the move toward more equitable standards-based grading?
- Katie and her team took advantage of the difficult circumstances of the pandemic to rethink and refine their approach to grading. When has a challenge in your professional career turned into an opportunity?

Challenges of the Technological Landscape

The transition to more equitable grading practices often faces significant technological challenges due to outdated or inflexible grading software and learning management systems. As a result, teachers can find themselves constrained by the existing infrastructure. These technological limitations frequently dictate grading practices. Although teachers develop rubrics and other assessment tools that align with equitable, standards-based grading practices, changes to the formal reporting structure—that is, what appears on students' report cards—lag behind. There is a disconnect between evolving assessment techniques and the rigid reporting structures imposed by existing systems. The tail of technology, unfortunately, often wags the dog of improved grading, evaluation, and teaching practices.

The educational technology landscape is in constant flux, with new software competitors and LMS options continually emerging. This can create confusion for educators and administrators alike as they attempt to select and implement systems that align with their grading philosophy. The rapid pace of change can also lead to hesitation in adopting new systems, as schools fear investing in solutions that may quickly become obsolete.

LMS and SMS Constraints

Many LMSs and student management systems (SMSs) were designed with traditional grading methods in mind, which can present significant challenges for educators transitioning to standards-based grading. These systems often struggle to accommodate nuanced requirements such as tracking multiple standards per assessment or monitoring student progress across various competencies over time. Although teachers may have a clear vision for implementing more equitable grading methods, the technological infrastructure regularly presents impediments. Educators find themselves creating makeshift solutions to bridge the gap between their grading philosophy and LMS and SMS capabilities—workarounds that can be time-consuming and confusing.

The discrepancy between aspirations for equitable grading practices and LMS and SMS technical capabilities can be unexpectedly frustrating. English teacher Jake Carlsen experienced this firsthand when attempting to implement a "no zeros" policy in his gradebook after being challenged to try it by someone at a district meeting. Jake says it took a year to set up "because we needed the IT team's help to modify the gradebook system. We needed to be able to mark assignments as missing rather than just assigning zeros." Jake's experience highlights how technical hurdles can delay or complicate the adoption of even seemingly simple equitable grading practices.

Reporting Challenges

Transforming detailed assessments of multiple standards into a cohesive grade report often requires navigating between standards-based assessment and familiar grading formats to satisfy institutional and parental demands. Science teacher Katie Linklater uses a four-point scale for her assessments, but her school's LMS gradebook is based on a 100-point system. "To bridge this gap," she reports, "I have to do conversions. I include a conversion chart in my syllabus that explains how Exceeding Standard or Meeting Standard translates into percentages in our LMS. For example, I'll tell students that if they get a 3 on an assignment, it goes into the system as 85 percent." The process adds a layer of complication to grade reporting.

Another significant issue arises from the difference between what students and parents see on a report card compared to teachers' access to assessment results. Although teachers may have a comprehensive view of student progress across multiple standards, web portals that allow students and their families to access their grades are often capable of conveying only a more simplified, traditional grade-based view. Adam Green describes the situation at his school: "The 'backside' display for students, parents, and caregivers in our system is different from what we as teachers see." This discrepancy can lead to confusion and misunderstandings about students' performance.

If these challenges could be overcome, what might standards-based grade reports look like? Figure 6.2 shows an example of a report card using the

FIGURE 6.2
Example of a Report Card Based on Most Recent Performance

Name: Tierney Bordeaux
Subject: Integrated Mathematics II

Standards Category	Most Recent Performance
Number and quantity operations	4 Excelling
Algebraic reasoning	4 Excelling
Geometric concepts	3 Proficient/Meets standard
Statistics and probability	4 Excelling
Mathematical modeling	3 Proficient/Meets standard

Final grade: A

Rationale: Tierney has demonstrated Excelling performance in three standards and Proficient performance in two standards. Based on the most recent performance levels and logic rules, Tierney has earned an *A*.

most recent performance grading method. The report, aligned with essential standards, directly ties grading to specific learning standards, providing both a clear indication of a student's current level of understanding for each standard and a holistic letter grade. Grade reports based on the standards could also be enhanced by progress visualization tools for a clear, graphical representation of a student's growth over time for each individual standard. Such visual aids would make it easier for teachers, students, and parents alike to understand current performance levels, track improvement, and identify areas that may need additional focus, ultimately fostering a more transparent and engaging grade-reporting experience.

Reporting Frequency Requirements

Another obstacle teachers face is the pressure to enter frequent grades because parents and caregivers want to be apprised in a timely way about student progress or missing work. Spanish teacher John Reafleng's principal required teachers to update their gradebooks frequently, but because he was prioritizing practice and formative assessment over recording grades, he tried to explain that there was nothing to enter. "She insisted I find something to grade," he recalls, "so I created low-stakes vocabulary quizzes. But the frequent grading requirement contradicts the time-saving benefits I expected from reducing participation, homework, and classwork grades."

Teachers may find themselves in the same boat as John. If so, low-stakes formative assessment tasks that can be recorded without heavily impacting final grades can include comprehension checks, exit tickets, and short quizzes on current material. Teachers can also enter completion marks for practice work in the gradebook, minimally weighting them or assigning them to a separate category so as not to affect final grade calculations.

Budget-Driven Decision Making

Unfortunately, decisions about which LMS a school uses are not always driven by pedagogical or equity-focused concerns. Budget limitations often play a significant role, forcing schools and districts to prioritize cost over functionality or alignment with grading philosophies. This can result in the implementation of systems that hinder rather than support the transition to more equitable grading practices. Michelle Hubbard, a high school French teacher, explains that, although her district previously had an LMS system that supported equitable grading, it switched to an outdated system, possibly for budget reasons. The "new" LMS does have a standards-based grading program available, but her district hasn't purchased this upgrade. "As a result, we're stuck using percentage-based grading," she says, "which creates problems for both students and teachers. I hope we can convince our superintendent and other decision makers to invest in a grading system that actually aligns with and supports the equitable practices they advocate for."

Overcoming Technological Barriers

Despite these challenges, innovative educators are finding ways to work within and around system limitations. Some are advocating for greater customization options within existing LMS platforms, whereas others are exploring alternative grading software that better aligns with equitable, standards-based grading principles. Collaboration among educators, IT professionals, and software developers will be crucial in bridging the gap between reforming grading policies and technological capabilities.

As the education community continues to push for more equitable grading practices, technology must evolve to support these efforts. This may involve developing more flexible LMS platforms that can accommodate different grading approaches; improving communication tools to better align teacher, student, and parent views of academic progress; creating professional learning opportunities to help teachers maximize the potential of their existing systems; and advocating for budget allocations that prioritize pedagogically sound technology solutions.

Let's consider a scenario where you are appointed to a school or district committee tasked with evaluating and recommending an LMS or SMS for adoption—similar to serving on a new textbook selection committee. What specific features or qualities should you prioritize in your evaluation process? What features of an LMS gradebook would best support teachers in implementing equitable grading practices, ultimately fostering a more accurate, motivating, and fair assessment system for all students? Figure 6.3 provides some criteria to consider.

Equitable, standards-based grading practices can be the tide that lifts all boats for all populations of students. As schools embrace this change, they may encounter challenges, but the potential benefits for student learning and

FIGURE 6.3
LMS Selection Criteria

Criteria	Description
Standards alignment	Allows teachers to easily tag assignments and assessments with specific learning standards or competencies
Flexible scoring scale	Implements a 4-point grading scale instead of the traditional 100-point system
Mastery tracking	Provides a clear view of student mastery levels for each standard over time, allowing teachers to monitor progress effectively
Separate formative and summative assessments	Enables teachers to distinguish between practice (formative) and final (summative) assessments in grade calculations
Multiple grading algorithms	Offers various grading methods (e.g., most recent, sustained progress, decaying average) to accurately represent student growth
Reassessment	Allows for easy recording and updating of grades when students retake assessments, without penalizing them for multiple attempts
Progress visualization	Includes tools for graphing or visually representing student progress on individual standards over time; incorporates student portfolios
Customizable rubrics	Provides the ability to create and use detailed rubrics aligned with essential standards
Exclusion of nonacademic factors	Allows exclusion of behavior, effort, or participation in academic grade calculations
Differentiated grouping	Facilitates creating student groups based on mastery levels to support differentiated instruction
Feedback mechanism	Incorporates a robust system for providing specific, actionable feedback on each essential standard or competency

(continued)

FIGURE 6.3
LMS Selection Criteria (Continued)

Criteria	Description
Standards summary	Offers the capability to summarize multiple essential standards into an overall grade for transcripts or eligibility purposes
Parent/student portal	Provides external users with a clear, standards-based view of progress, aligning with the teacher's perspective
Data analysis	Tools include features for analyzing student performance data to inform instruction and identify learning gaps
Customizable reporting	Allows for flexible, standards-based report card generation that accurately reflects student learning

equity are significant. Kim Haber eloquently captures the positive impact of this transition: "Our new system has transformed our learning environment. Instead of asking for extra points, students now focus on improving specific skills. This shift changes the 'learning currency' from arbitrary points to concrete knowledge and skills—a significant improvement."

Pause and Reflect

Take a look at the following prompts and select a couple that are relevant to you based on where you are regarding the grading and reporting issues discussed in this chapter. Reflect on your own, discuss with colleagues one-on-one, or start a discussion with your team.

- How does your current gradebook system align with or diverge from standards-based grading principles? What specific changes could you implement to make your grading practices more equitable and reflective of student learning?
- Which grading method—most recent, sustained progress, logic rules, or decaying average—might be most appropriate for your subject area

and students? How could you explain how it works and get buy-in from students, families, and administrators?
- What challenges do you anticipate in transitioning to a more equitable grading system using your school's current LMS? How might you work around these limitations or advocate for necessary changes?
- If you were on a selection committee for a new LMS, which features would you prioritize to support equitable and standards-based grading practices in your school or district?

7

Schoolwide Implementation of New Grading Practices

Creating Consistency Across Classrooms

Picture this: You are having lunch in your classroom, going over your lesson plan for your next class, and in walks a colleague you are only distantly acquainted with. He proceeds to confront you—in a polite but insistent way—about your flexible deadlines policy, claiming that it undermines his own zero-tolerance policy for late work when students expect the same "leniency" from him. You tell him that you acknowledge his concerns and explain the research-based reasons that you've decided to prioritize students' mastery of content and skills over their ability to meet arbitrary deadlines. "That sounds good in theory," he says, "but I'm the one dealing with angry parents who don't understand why their child got a zero in my class when they can turn in work whenever they want in yours. It's creating inconsistency across the school."

"That's not quite how the policy works," you respond, "but I see your point about inconsistency. Perhaps we could bring this up at the next staff meeting? It might be beneficial to have a schoolwide conversation about our grading practices and how we can align them better while still meeting students' needs."

Resolving Conflicts in Philosophy

Implementing innovative grading practices that truly reflect student learning and empower students in their education can clash with established norms.

Teachers wedded to traditional grading practices can feel isolated—as can the teachers trying to implement new approaches within a traditional environment. Spanish teacher Osvaldo Díaz had the latter experience at two schools, telling us that the lack of support "consistently hindered my ability to fully implement and advocate for equitable grading practices." Reform-minded teachers often face resistance from colleagues, skepticism from parents and administrators, and confusion from students trying to meet inconsistent expectations.

A lack of schoolwide alignment in grading practices can create tension among staff and limit the benefits of these approaches. Students may receive different grades in different classes for similar levels of learning, undermining fairness and reliability. Tensions can arise between teachers with differing grading philosophies. Parents might struggle to understand varying grading systems, while administrators find it challenging to interpret conflicting grading data. These inconsistencies can undermine the credibility of the school's assessment practices in general and hamper efforts to ensure equitable education. As Conor O'Brien, a social studies teacher, observes, "Aligning grading practices across a department and school would reduce confusion for students and make our jobs easier." Despite these challenges, many early adopters persist in pursuing reformation, knowing that equitable grading will better serve students' learning needs and promote equity.

How can teachers shift a school's grading culture to promote equity, consistency, and fairness in student evaluation? The first step is to seek out like-minded colleagues in your professional learning community, grade-level team, or department—leveraging the power of these groups to introduce grading innovations that complement ongoing work, reinforce shared values, and inspire better student performance through clear expectations and enhanced motivation.

Professional Learning Communities

Professional learning communities (PLCs) are collaborative teams that support educators to improve teaching and student learning outcomes. These teacher teams provide an ideal platform for introducing grading innovations that complement ongoing work.

Reform-minded teachers can work with their PLC to propose integrating rubrics into existing common summative assessments, initiating discussions about learning objectives, success criteria, and consistent evaluation methods. PLC members can collaborate to align evaluations more effectively and conduct calibration sessions for common assessments, ensuring consistency and fairness in analyzing and scoring. Science teacher Tim Larsen recalls, "All of us came with samples of labs from each of our classes, and we looked at their proficiency levels. It was really helpful for me to refine my rating." Regular calibration promotes skill articulation, maintains grading uniformity, identifies discrepancies, and strengthens collaborative culture (Kollman, 2024). The process also improves grading accuracy and can lead to deeper conversations about grading philosophies, equity, and assessment purpose, potentially inspiring more comprehensive reforms over time.

Departmental Teams

Another good place to start any kind of schoolwide reform is at the departmental level. Teachers who are pursuing innovative grading practices can share their experiences and data with departmental colleagues to persuade them to join the cause. Following are some things you can present to garner support:

- **Learning outcomes:** Share data on student achievement (e.g., improved test scores, increased mastery of key concepts), comparing results before and after implementing the new grading policy.
- **Grade distribution:** Demonstrate how the new policy has affected overall grade distribution, potentially showing a more accurate representation of student learning.
- **Student feedback:** Share student comments on the perceived fairness of the new system and its effects on their stress levels and motivation to learn and improve.
- **Workload management:** Discuss how the policy has affected your workload, potentially freeing up time for more meaningful feedback and instruction.
- **Alignment with standards:** Explain how the new grading practices better align with content standards and learning objectives.

Communicating about concrete evidence and personal experiences can spark meaningful discussions about grading practices within departments and prompt reflection on what works and what doesn't. "That's the way we improve as professionals," says Osvaldo Díaz. These kinds of conversations can also help address concerns and misconceptions about grading reform while highlighting the benefits. Colleagues may find performance data and actual student commentary more thought-provoking and convincing than another teacher's opinion or the prescription from an educational expert they heard at a summer training. As more teachers within the department adopt similar practices, it can create a ripple effect, eventually leading to schoolwide conversations about grading policies and potential reforms.

Leveraging Teacher Leadership and Administrative Support

The implementation of schoolwide equity grading initiatives is most effective when it emerges from the grassroots efforts of passionate and informed teachers. The key to successful and lasting reform lies in the leadership of interested teachers and teacher leaders (Stanulis et al., 2024). These educators on the front lines of instruction and assessment have the most intimate understanding of the challenges and opportunities presented by current grading practices. Their firsthand experiences and insights are invaluable in shaping and implementing effective, equitable grading strategies.

The importance of teacher-led initiatives cannot be overstated. Hargreaves and Fullan (2012) note that school reforms that originate from the ground up tend to be more successful and sustainable than top-down mandates for several reasons:

- **Authenticity:** Teacher-led initiatives are rooted in real classroom experiences and challenges, making them more relevant and practical.
- **Buy-in:** When teachers lead the change, their colleagues are more likely to embrace and support the new practices because they trust the judgment of their peers (and are more skeptical about edicts from above).
- **Adaptability:** Teacher-driven reforms can be more easily adapted to the specific needs and context of individual schools or departments.
- **Sustainability:** Changes that are driven by teachers are more likely to persist over time because they become embedded in the school culture rather than being seen as an external imposition.

- **Professional growth:** Leading change initiatives provides valuable opportunities for teacher leadership and professional development.

That said, teachers cannot truly effect change without administrative support. Educators interested in grading reform must be able to effectively communicate to administrators the benefits not only for individual students but also for the whole school. The positive consequences of schoolwide equitable grading policies—such as increased graduation rates, improved college readiness, and a more inclusive school culture—affect students of all demographics. Administrators can play a crucial role in supporting teacher-led initiatives by (1) providing resources and time for professional development, (2) facilitating communication among different departments and grade levels, (3) aligning equitable grading practices with district and state policies, and (4) communicating the importance of these changes to parents and the broader community. By empowering teachers to drive these reforms, school leaders can create a powerful synergy between bottom-up innovation and top-down support.

Raising Awareness Through Book Studies

Book studies on equitable grading (by authors such as Ken O'Connor, Starr Sackstein, Joe Feldman, Cathy Vatterott, and Rick Wormeli) can be another effective way to introduce and implement equitable grading strategies, especially in schools where departmental structures or small school sizes may limit organic conversations about reform. This text-focused approach allows interested teachers to explore and pilot new grading methods in a supportive, collaborative environment.

Book study participants attend regular meetings over the course of a semester or school year to discuss content, share insights, and explore how concepts studied apply to their classroom contexts. This collaborative approach allows for rich discussions and the exchange of ideas across different subject areas and grade levels. As the group progresses through the text, they can begin to identify specific grading strategies they wish to pilot in their classrooms. For example, they might explore implementing standards-based grading, eliminating penalties for late work, or providing opportunities for reassessment. The book study format provides a supportive environment for teachers to share their experiences, challenges, and successes with these new approaches.

To enhance the impact of the book study, participants can engage in a variety of activities to deepen their understanding and implementation of equitable grading:

- **Reflect on current grading practices and biases.** Critically examine your existing grading methods, identifying potential inequities or unconscious biases. For example, you might realize you have been grading participation based on hand raising, which may disadvantage introverted students or those from cultures that value different forms of engagement.
- **Experiment with new grading strategies.** Implement novel approaches learned from the book study. For instance, you might try a system where students can retake tests after receiving additional instruction, focusing on mastery rather than a single point-in-time assessment.
- **Collect data on student performance and engagement.** Use an action research approach to gather quantitative and qualitative data to assess the impact of new grading practices. This might include tracking changes in grade distributions, conducting student surveys on their perception of fairness, or documenting changes in homework completion rates.
- **Create a digital platform to share resources and experiences.** Establish a shared online space for the book study group such as a Google Drive folder or a dedicated Slack channel. Members can upload relevant articles, share lesson plans incorporating equitable grading principles, or post reflections on their implementation journey.
- **Share successes and challenges with the group.** Regular meetings can serve as a forum for participants to discuss their experiences. A science teacher might share how eliminating penalties for late work has increased overall assignment completion, whereas an English teacher might seek advice on managing the increased workload from offering more frequent reassessment opportunities.

As teachers participating in the book study experience success and share their insights with colleagues, interest in equitable grading may grow organically within the school community. This teacher-driven approach can be particularly effective in fostering lasting change, as it allows teachers to take ownership of the process and adapt practices to their specific needs and contexts.

Spotlight: Effecting Systemic Change
Michelle Hubbard, French, Santa Cruz High School
Santa Cruz, California

For years, Michelle and some of her colleagues in the world languages department had been making strides toward equitable grading reform through such practices as offering students opportunities to retake exams during the lunch period and reducing the weight of formative assessments in grade calculation.

However, the catalyst for systemic change at Michelle's high school took the form of a new principal's invitation to the teacher leadership team to do a book study focused on equitable grading practices. Inspired by what they learned from the study, teacher PLCs began work on establishing essential or power standards. A "grading inquiry" group of teacher leaders from each academic department (including Michelle) identified steps toward implementing standards-based grading. They conducted teacher surveys to understand which equity grading practices teachers were considering adopting. Conor O'Brien, another teacher in the group, described their process: "Our goal was to integrate retakes, an easily adoptable practice, into all classrooms. . . . Last year, our main focus was on determining how to convince other educators to adopt these practices and deciding which ones to prioritize."

This teacher-by-teacher approach to school change allowed for personalized guidance and addressed individual concerns. In communicating the new practices to stakeholders, the school opted to describe it as "equitable grading"—terminology that helped emphasize the focus on fairness and student success. Michelle recalled, "By reframing our initiative as a shift toward 'equitable grading' rather than 'standards-based grading,' we found that this simple change in terminology could significantly alter mindsets and increase acceptance of the reform." This helped clarify teachers' goals and increased acceptance of the reform.

Transforming grading practices schoolwide also included a structural change in the school schedule: the addition of a special period each week where teachers could provide tutoring and in-class time for students to prepare for and take reassessments. This modification demonstrated the school's commitment to supporting all students in their learning journey.

To support and engage her students in the new protocols around grading, Michelle shares with them both the importance of practice activities and their minimal weight in comparison with summative assessments. She explains how she plans to track what she terms "habits of work and citizenship" and invites students to discuss behaviors and activities that lead to success in class, including attendance and engagement, active participation, completing practice work and homework, feedback, and reflection. This approach reinforces the validity of grades for evaluating student learning while recognizing the importance of developing beneficial work habits.

Reflecting on the journey, Michelle sees her school's transformation as a gradual but significant shift in education philosophy and practice. What began as isolated efforts in her department has evolved into a schoolwide equitable grading initiative that is currently progressing to include the entire district. As the reform gained traction, Michelle's role became increasingly central to this system's change. She was asked to provide professional development on equity grading not only to teacher teams at her high school but also for the County Office of Education. The process has required patience, persistence, and a willingness to engage in difficult conversations about fairness and student success. As the district moves closer to implementing districtwide standards, though, Michelle remains committed to the cause, recognizing the potential for these changes to create a sustainable, more equitable, more effective learning environment for all students.

Spotlight Questions

- What does Michelle's story illustrate about the importance of reform movements coming from the bottom up (as opposed to top down)? What might have happened if, instead of grading reform stemming from teacher involvement, a district administrator or principal had decided to mandate equity grading practices across the board?
- What are some of the benefits and drawbacks to the teacher-by-teacher approach taken by the grading inquiry committee?

Integrating Equitable Grading with Other Practices

Schools that are already implementing social and emotional learning (SEL) and trauma-informed and culturally responsive practices are ripe for integrating equitable assessment strategies. These practices share common objectives of supporting student well-being, fostering resilience, and developing problem-solving skills and student agency—skills that have been identified by both employers and new hires as lacking in the workforce (Anderson & Winthrop, 2025). By aligning equitable grading with established frameworks, schools can create a holistic, comprehensive, and effective approach to student support and achievement, ultimately both promoting equity in education and better preparing students for future success.

The first step in integrating equity grading practices with SEL, trauma-sensitive, and culturally responsive approaches is to recognize how the origins and trajectories of all three intersect and develop a shared understanding and vision among educators, administrators, and other stakeholders (Osher et al., 2021). This involves recognizing the complementary nature of these approaches and how they collectively contribute to creating safe, equitable, and engaging learning environments.

Social and Emotional Learning

Aligning equitable grading with core SEL competencies such as self-awareness, self-management, social awareness, relationship skills, and responsible decision making (CASEL, n.d.) can enhance students' skills in those areas, enabling them to better reflect on their learning progress and set meaningful goals for improvement. This alignment empowers students to take a more active role in their educational journey.

The implementation of transparent and fair grading practices fosters stronger, more trusting relationships between students and teachers, directly supporting the SEL domains of social awareness and relationship skills. This improved dynamic can lead to a more positive and supportive classroom environment where students feel valued and understood.

Additionally, equitable grading practices that encourage students to take greater responsibility for their learning through self-assessment, tracking their own learning, and setting personal goals for improvement reinforce the SEL competency of responsible decision making. Providing multiple chances for success and emphasizing growth over static achievement helps students develop resilience and a growth mindset, key factors in both academic success and personal development. This integrated approach creates a more holistic and supportive educational experience that addresses both academic achievement and social-emotional well-being.

Trauma-Informed Practices

Equity grading practices naturally align with trauma-informed approaches by recognizing and addressing the diverse needs and experiences of students and creating safe and supportive environments where students feel capable of success. Grading practices such as eliminating punitive measures for late work can help prevent school-related trauma and support students who may be dealing with adverse experiences outside school. This approach also aids in avoiding retraumatization, which is crucial for students who have experienced trauma. Providing multiple opportunities for success and focusing on growth rather than punishment also supports the development of resilience, a key aspect of both SEL and trauma-informed approaches (Portell, 2021).

Culturally Responsive Teaching

The integration of equitable and standards-based grading practices also dovetails with culturally responsive teaching. Offering multiple assessment options (e.g., oral presentations, written essays, multimedia projects) allows students to show what they know in ways that reflect their strengths and preferences. This approach also respects the varied learning styles and communication methods present in a diverse classroom.

Practices such as not grading on participation or attendance and not penalizing late work support students who may come from cultural backgrounds that differ from the mainstream. Using inclusive and culturally responsive language in assignments and grading criteria helps minimize potential biases in subjective assessments of student conduct (Feldman, 2019a). Inclusive classroom practices such as cooperative learning structures and peer feedback opportunities, which allow students to interact with and learn from peers of diverse backgrounds (Yoder et al., 2021), support all students' success.

Multitiered System of Supports

A multitiered system of supports (MTSS) is a framework that provides a data-driven structure to address student needs across academic, behavioral, and social-emotional domains. Incorporating equitable grading practices within this tiered system facilitates culturally responsive and fair assessment and supportive intervention strategies for all students.

Schools can use MTSS data to analyze student performance patterns across support tiers and evaluate the effects of grading practices on various student groups. This analysis may reveal disparities in intervention effectiveness or highlight how specific grading practices disproportionately affect students receiving Tier 2 or Tier 3 supports. For example, data showing that historically disadvantaged students are overrepresented in upper-tier supports and predominantly enrolled in classes using traditional grading practices would provide compelling evidence of a need for schoolwide assessment reform. Over time, equitable grading practices could become part of Tier 1 support for all students and be incorporated into students' individualized education programs and 504 plans.

By aligning equitable grading practices with MTSS structures, schools can develop a holistic view of student needs and strengths, facilitating targeted, culturally responsive interventions that address the whole child while enriching school culture. This integrated approach promotes equity, supports trauma-informed practices, and fosters social-emotional development while maintaining a focus on data-driven decision making and continuous improvement.

Shifting the Professional Mindset

As schools continue this work, those involved must regularly assess the effect of newly integrated practices and make adjustments as needed to best serve all students. This requires educators to reflect on their biases and beliefs about student capabilities in order to develop essential self-awareness. Teacher leaders, instructional coaches, and staff can advocate for ongoing professional development that integrates equitable grading with existing frameworks and practices. Successful implementation of new grading approaches necessitates strong administrative support, underscoring the importance of leadership engagement in this process.

Schools that successfully integrate standards-based grading with other supportive frameworks have the potential to become model institutions, serving as demonstration sites for public school districts or independent school regional associations. Exemplary schools can showcase the practical implementation and positive outcomes of integrated equitable grading practices, providing valuable insights and inspiration for other education institutions seeking to embark on a journey of reform. These schools can also serve as clinical practice sites for schools of education, offering teacher candidates hands-on experience with innovative, equitable grading practices—thus equipping the next generation of educators with the knowledge and skills to implement fair and effective assessment strategies in their classrooms. Embracing these comprehensive approaches to grading reform will result in schools that are supportive, equitable, and effective learning environments that prepare all students for success in an increasingly complex world.

Remember why you began this journey: to make a difference in the lives of students. By courageous reflection, sustained effort, and a willingness to evolve your assessment practices, you are not only opening new possibilities for each learner in your care but also becoming part of a larger movement to transform education for the better. The hard work is worth it—because when assessment is anchored in equity, every student has the opportunity to succeed and educators reclaim the power to truly serve, uplift, and inspire the next generation.

Pause and Reflect

Take a look at the following prompts and select a couple that are relevant to you based on where you and your students are regarding implementing equitable grading practices schoolwide. Reflect on your own, discuss with colleagues one-on-one, or start a discussion with your team.

- Where would you rate your school in terms of developing coherent schoolwide equity grading practices: Beginning, Developing, Proficient, or Advanced? What are some of your observations that explain your rating?
- Which of the established structures discussed in this chapter do you think lend themselves the most to work that could expand or refine the use of equitable grading practices at your school or in your district? What might be some next steps for you?
- What challenges to schoolwide or districtwide grading reform (or even to refining your current practice) do you envision? What do you want to keep in mind to help you overcome these challenges?

References

Alvarez, B. (2024, April 16). Disproportionality in special education fueled by implicit bias. *NEA Today.* https://www.nea.org/nea-today/all-news-articles/disproportionality-special-education-fueled-implicit-bias

Anderson, J., & Winthrop, R. (2025). *The disengaged teen: Helping kids learn better, feel better, and live better.* Penguin Random House.

Anderson, M. (2019). *What we say and how we say it matter: Teacher talk that improves student learning and behavior.* ASCD.

Andrade, H. L., & Brookhart, S. M. (2020). Classroom assessment as the co-regulation of learning. *Assessment in Education: Principles, Policy & Practice, 27*(4), 350–372.

Arter, J., & McTighe, J. (2001). *Scoring rubrics in the classroom: Using performance criteria for assessing and improving student performance.* Corwin.

Atwell, N. (1987). *In the middle: Writing, reading, and learning with adolescents.* Boynton/Cook.

Berwick, C. (2022, September 30). Fact check: Are flexible student deadlines at odds with real life? *Edutopia.* https://www.edutopia.org/article/fact-check-are-flexible-student-deadlines-odds-real-life

Brookhart, S. M. (2008). *How to give effective feedback to your students.* ASCD.

Brookhart, S. M. (2011). Starting the conversation about grading. *Educational Leadership, 69*(3), 10–14. https://www.ascd.org/el/articles/starting-the-conversation-about-grading

Brookhart, S. M. (2013). *How to create and use rubrics for formative assessment and grading.* ASCD.

Brookhart, S. M. (2018). Appropriate criteria: Key to effective rubrics. *Frontiers in Education, 3,* 22.

Brookhart, S. M., & Chen, F. (2015). The quality and effectiveness of descriptive rubrics. *Educational Review, 67*(3), 343–368.

Butler, R. (1988). Enhancing and undermining intrinsic motivation: The effects of task-involving and ego-involving evaluation on interest and performance. *British Journal of Educational Psychology, 58*(1), 1–14.

Butler, R., & Nisan, M. (1986). Effects of no feedback, task-related comments, and grades on intrinsic motivation and performance. *Journal of Educational Psychology, 78*(3), 210–216.

Cain, S. (2012). *Quiet: The power of introverts in a world that can't stop talking*. Crown.

Carifio, J., & Carey, T. (2009). A critical examination of current minimum grading policy recommendations. *The High School Journal, 93*(1), 23–37.

CDC. (2024). *Youth mental health: The numbers*. https://www.cdc.gov/healthy-youth/mental-health/mental-health-numbers.html

Challenge Success. (2020, August). *Quality over quantity: Elements of effective homework*. https://challengesuccess.org/wp-content/uploads/2021/04/Challenge-Success-Homework-White-Paper-2020.pdf

Chamberlin, K., Yasué, M., & Chiang, I.-C. A. (2023). The impact of grades on student motivation. *Active Learning in Higher Education, 24*(2), 109–124.

Chen, C.-H., & Yang, Y.-C. (2019). Revisiting the effects of project-based learning on students' academic achievement: A meta-analysis investigating moderators. *Educational Research Review, 26*, 71–81.

Chen, L., Chen, P., & Lin, Z. (2020). Artificial intelligence in education: A review. *IEEE Access, 8*, 75264–75278.

Cherng, H.-Y. S. (2017). If they think I can: Teacher bias and youth of color expectations and achievement. *Social Science Research, 66*, 170–186.

Christopher, S. (2007). Homework: A few practice arrows. *Educational Leadership, 65*(4). https://www.ascd.org/el/articles/homework-a-few-practice-arrows

Collaborative for Academic, Social, and Emotional Learning (CASEL). (n.d.). *Fundamentals of SEL*. https://casel.org/fundamentals-of-sel

Conley, D. T. (2010). *College and career ready: Helping all students succeed beyond high school* (1st ed.). Jossey-Bass.

Darbyshire, J. (2023, March). *International Women's Day 2023 — Equity*. Charterhouse. https://www.charterhouse.com.au/blog/2023/03/international-womens-day-2023-equity

Darling-Hammond, L. (2001). Inequality in teaching and schooling: How opportunity is rationed to students of color in America. In B. D. Smedley, A. Y. Stith, L. Colburn, & C. H. Evans (Eds.), *The right thing to do, the smart thing to do: Enhancing diversity in the health professions* (pp. 208–203). National Academy Press: Institute of Medicine.

Deci, E. L., & Ryan, R. M. (2000). The "what" and "why" of goal pursuits: Human needs and the self determination of behavior. *Psychology Inquiry, 11*(4), 227–268.

Delpit, L. (2012). *"Multiplication is for white people": Raising expectations for other people's children*. New Press.

Dewey, J. (1916). *Democracy and education: An introduction to the philosophy of education*. Macmillan.

Dewey, J. (1938). *Experience and education*. Macmillan.

Dlaska, A., & Krekeler, C. (2017). Does grading undermine feedback? The influence of grades on the effectiveness of corrective feedback on L2 writing. *The Language Learning Journal, 45*(2), 185–201.

Downey, D. B., & Pribesh, S. (2004). When race matters: Teachers' evaluations of students' classroom behavior. *Sociology of Education, 77*(4), 267–282.

Duckor, B., & Holmberg, C. (2024). Engaging, motivating, and supporting students through feedback. *Phi Delta Kappan, 105*(5), 46–53.

Dweck, C. S. (2006). *Mindset: The new psychology of success*. Random House.

Engel, S. (2015). *The hungry mind: The origins of curiosity in childhood*. Harvard University Press.

Ertmer, P. A., & Simons, K. D. (2006). Jumping the PBL implementation hurdle: Supporting the efforts of K–12 teachers. *The Interdisciplinary Journal of Problem-Based Learning*, 1(1), 40–54.

Feldman, J. (2019a, January 23). What traditional classroom grading gets wrong. *Education Week*. https://www.edweek.org/teaching-learning/opinion-what-traditional-classroom-grading-gets-wrong/2019/01

Feldman, J. (2019b). *Grading for equity: What it is, why it matters, and how it can transform schools and classrooms* (1st ed.). Corwin.

Feldman, J. (2020). Taking the stress out of grading. *Educational Leadership*, 78(1). https://www.ascd.org/el/articles/taking-the-stress-out-of-grading

Feldman, J. (2024a, July 30). *Can we trust the transcript? Recognizing student potential through more accurate grading*. Crescendo Education Group. https://crescendoedgroup.org/blog/equitable-grading/can-we-trust-the-transcript

Feldman, J. (2024b). *Grading for equity: What it is, why it matters, and how it can transform schools and classrooms* (2nd ed.). Corwin.

Feldman, J., & Reed Marshall, T. (2020). Empowering students by demystifying grading. *Educational Leadership*, 77(6). https://www.ascd.org/el/articles/empowering-students-by-demystifying-grading

Fisher, D., & Frey, N. (2021). *Better learning through structured teaching: A framework for the gradual release of responsibility* (3rd ed.). ASCD.

Fleishman, T. (2024, March 22). Flexible due dates lower stress without loss of rigor. *Cornell Chronicle*. https://news.cornell.edu/stories/2024/03/flexible-due-dates-lower-student-stress-without-loss-rigor

Frey, N., Fisher, D., & Hattie, J. (2018). Developing "assessment capable" learners. *Educational Leadership*, 75(5), 46–51. https://ascd.org/el/articles/developing-assessment-capable-learners

Gkintoni, E., Dimakos, I., Halkiopoulos, C., & Antonopoulou, H. (2023). Contributions of neuroscience to educational praxis: A systematic review. *Emerging Science Journal*, 7, 146–158.

Gladwell, M. (2008). *Outliers: The story of success*. Little Brown.

Gonzalez, J. (n.d.). *A few ideas for dealing with late work*. Cult of Pedagogy. https://www.cultofpedagogy.com/late-work

Great Schools Partnership. (n.d.). Grading and reporting for educational equity. Proficiency-based grading. https://www.greatschoolspartnership.org/proficiency-based-learning/grading-reporting

Guo, J., & Ji, H. (2019). The potential and challenges of using artificial intelligence in education. *International Journal of Information and Education Technology*, 9(9), 631–636.

Guskey, T. R. (2013). The case against percentage grades. *Educational Leadership*, 71(1), 68–72. https://www.ascd.org/el/articles/the-case-against-percentage-grades

Guskey, T. R. (2015). *On your mark: Challenging the conventions of grading and reporting*. Solution Tree.

Guskey, T. R. (2021). Learning from failures: Lessons from unsuccessful grading reform initiatives. *NASSP Bulletin*, 105(3), 192–199.

Guskey, T. (2022, October 24). Can grades be an effective form of freedom? *Kappan Online*. https://doi.org/10.3102/1888328

Guskey, T. R., Fisher, D., & Frey, N. (2024). The unwinnable battle over minimum grades. *Educational Leadership*, 82(2). ASCD. https://www.ascd.org/el/articles/the-unwinnable-battle-over-minimum-grades

Hammond, Z. (2014). *Culturally responsive teaching and the brain: Promoting authentic engagement and rigor among culturally and linguistically diverse students*. Corwin.

Hammond, Z. (2015, February 26). Making CRT manageable. *Culturally responsive teaching and the brain*. https://crtandthebrain.com/making-crt-manageable

Hammond, Z. (2018). Culturally responsive teaching puts rigor at the center. *The Learning Professional*, 39(5), 40–43.

Hammond, Z. (2020). The power of protocols for equity. *Educational Leadership*, 77(7). https://www.ascd.org/el/articles/the-power-of-protocols-for-equity

Hargreaves, A., & Fullan, M. (2012). *Professional capital: Transforming teaching in every school*. Teachers College Press.

Hattie, J., & Timperley, H. (2007). The power of feedback. *Review of Educational Research*, 77(1), 81–112.

Hawlitschek, A. (2017). Feedback in educational computer games: A systematic review. *International Journal of Serious Games*, 4(1), 39–60.

Heritage, M. (2007). Formative assessment: What do teachers need to know and do? *Phi Delta Kappan*, 89(2), 140–145.

Hills, M., & Peacock, K. (2022). Replacing power with flexible structure: Implementing flexible deadlines to improve student learning experiences. *Teaching and Learning Inquiry*, 10, 1–15.

Hough, L. (2019, May 28). Grade expectations: Why we need to rethink grading in our schools. *Ed. Magazine*. https://www.gse.harvard.edu/ideas/ed-magazine/19/05/grade-expectations

Ickes, R. (2024, November 6). How I teach science like a sport. *SmartBrief*. https://www.smartbrief.com/original/how-i-teach-science-like-a-sport

Jönsson, A., & Panadero, E. (2017). The use and design of rubrics to support assessment for learning. In D. Carless, S. M. Bridges, C. K. Y. Chan, & R. Glofcheski (Eds.), *Scaling up assessment for learning in higher education* (pp. 99–111). Springer.

Jung, L. A., & Guskey, T. R. (2010). Grading exceptional learners. *Educational Leadership*, 67(5), 31–35. https://www.ascd.org/el/articles/grading-exceptional-learners

Kilgour, P., Northcote, M., Williams, A., & Kilgour, A. (2020). A plan for the co-construction and collaborative use of rubrics for student learning. *Assessment & Evaluation in Higher Education*, 45(1), 140–153.

Kingston, S. (2018). Project based learning & student achievement: What does the research tell us? *PBL Evidence Matters*, 1(1), 1–11. https://files.eric.ed.gov/fulltext/ED590832.pdf

Klapp, T., Klapp, A., & Gustafsson, J. E. (2024). Relations between students' well-being and academic achievement: Evidence from Swedish compulsory school. *European Journal of Psychology of Education*, 39, 275–296.

Kleinfeld, J. (1975). Effective teachers of Eskimo and Indian students. *The School Review*, 83(2), 301–344.

Kohn, A. (2011). The case against grades. *Educational Leadership*, 69(3). https://www.ascd.org/el/articles/the-case-against-grades

Kollman, A. (2024, July 5). 4 crucial steps for calibrating assessments. *Edutopia.* https://www.edutopia.org/article/importance-calibrating-assessments

Kuepper-Tetzel, C. E., & Gardner, P. L. (2021). Effects of temporary mark withholding on academic performance. *Psychology Learning & Teaching, 20*(3), 405–419.

Lamb, R. L., Annetta, L., Firestone, J., & Etopio, E. (2018). A meta-analysis with examination of moderators of student cognition, affect, and learning outcomes while using serious educational games, serious games, and simulations. *Computers in Human Behavior, 80,* 158–167.

Leslie, H. J. (2021). *Research on effects of grading.* University of San Diego Learning Design Center: Staff Scholarship. https://digital.sandiego.edu/ldc-scholarship/7

Lozano, L. M., García-Cueto, E., & Muñiz, J. (2008). The case against percentage grades. *Educational Leadership, 71*(1), 68–72.

Macrine, S. L., & Fugate, J. M. B. (2021). Translating embodied cognition for embodied learning in the classroom. *Frontiers in Education, 6.*

Marzano, R. J. (2010). *Formative assessment & standards-based grading.* Marzano Research Laboratory. Solution Tree.

Matteucci, M. C., Steuer, G., & Majcík, M. (2024). Mistakes in teaching and learning: Editorial. *Studia Paedagogica, 29*(2), 5–8. https://hdl.handle.net/11222.digilib/digilib.80621

McMillan, J. H., & Hearn, J. (2008). Student self-assessment: The key to stronger student motivation and higher achievement. *Educational Horizons, 87*(1), 40–49.

McTighe, J., & Tucker, C. (2022). Developing self-directed learners by design. *Educational Leadership, 80*(3). https://www.ascd.org/el/articles/developing-self-directed-learners-by-design

Narciss, S., & Alemdag, E. (2024). Learning from errors and failure in educational contexts: New insights and future directions for research and practice. *British Journal of Educational Psychology, 95*(1), 197–218.

O'Connor, K. (2011). *A repair kit for grading: 15 fixes for broken grades* (2nd ed.). Pearson.

Orttel, A. (2023). *Throwing away the late work penalty* (Master's thesis). Minnesota State University, Moorhead. *Dissertations, Theses, and Projects,* 768. https://red.mnstate.edu/thesis/768/

Osher, D., Guarino, K., Jones, W., & Schanfield, M. (2021). *Trauma-sensitive schools and social and emotional learning: An integration* [Issue brief]. Edna Bennett Pierce Prevention Research Center, The Pennsylvania State University. https://prevention.psu.edu/wp-content/uploads/2022/05/TSS-SEL-Brief-Final-June2021R.pdf

Panadero, E., & Jönsson, A. (2013). The use of scoring rubrics for formative assessment purposes revisited: A review. *Educational Research Review, 9,* 129–144.

Panadero, E., Jönsson, A., Pinedo, L., Fernández-Castilla, B. (2023). Effects of rubrics on academic performance, self-regulated learning, and self-efficacy: A meta-analytic review. *Educational Psychology Review, 35,* 113.

Panadero, E., & Romero, M. (2014). To rubric or not to rubric? The effects of self-assessment on self-regulation, performance and self-efficacy. *Assessment in Education: Principles, Policy & Practice, 21*(2), 133–148.

Patrick, K., Socol, A. R., & Morgan, I. (2020). *Inequities in advanced coursework* [Report]. EdTrust. https://edtrust.org/rti/inequities-in-advanced-coursework

PBLWorks. (n.d.). *What is PBL?* https://www.pblworks.org/what-is-pbl

Portell, M. (2021, October 13). Harnessing the synergy between trauma-informed teaching and SEL. *Edutopia*. https://www.edutopia.org/article/harnessing-synergy-between-trauma-informed-teaching-and-sel

Preston, C. C., & Colman, A. M. (2000). Optimal number of response categories in rating scales: Reliability, validity, discriminating power, and respondent preferences. *Acta Psychologica, 104*(1), 1–15.

Rebora, A. (2022). Shifting the "cognitive load" in classrooms. *Educational Leadership, 80*(3). https://ascd.org/el/articles/shifting-the-cognitive-load-in-classrooms

Reeves, D. B. (2004). The case against the zero. *Phi Delta Kappan, 86*(4), 324–325.

Reeves, D. B. (2006). Power standards: How leaders add value to state and national standards. In *The Jossey-Bass Reader on Educational Leadership* (p. 239). Jossey-Bass.

Robbins, Z. S. (2025, March 19). Correcting for implicit bias in grading. *Edutopia*. https://www.edutopia.org/article/implicit-bias-grading

Ryan, R. M., & Deci, E. L. (2017). *Self-determination theory: Basic psychological needs in motivation, development, and wellness*. Guilford.

Sadler, R. D. (1989). Formative assessment and the design of instructional systems. *Instructional Science, 18*, 119–144.

Schinske, J., & Tanner, K. (2014). Teaching more by grading less (or differently). *CBE Life Sciences Education, 13*(2), 159–166.

Schmoker, M. (2006). *Results now: How we can achieve unprecedented improvements in teaching and learning*. ASCD.

Schmoker, M. (2018). *Focus: Elevating the essentials to radically improve student learning*. ASCD.

Soncini, A., Visintin, E. P., Matteucci, M. C., Tomasetto, C., & Butera, F. (2022). Positive error climate promotes learning outcomes through students' adaptive reactions towards errors. *Learning and Instruction, 80*, 101627.

Spector, J. M., & Ma, S. (2019). Inquiry and critical thinking skills for the next generation: From artificial intelligence back to human intelligence. *Smart Learning Environments, 6*, 8.

Stanulis, R. N., Cooper, K. S., & Richard-Todd, R. R. (2024). Teacher-led reforms have a big advantage—Teachers. *Phi Delta Kappan, 97*(7), 53–57.

Stenhouse Publishers. (2010). *Rick Wormeli: Redos, retakes, and do-overs, part two* [Video]. YouTube. https://www.youtube.com/watch?v=wgxvzEc0rvs

Stiggins, R. J. (2012). Quality feedback. *Educational Leadership, 54*(7). https://www.ascd.org/el/articles/quality-feedback

Sweller, J. (2022). *Cognitive load theory: A teacher's guide*. Structural Learning. https://www.structural-learning.com/post/cognitive-load-theory-a-teachers-guide

Talbert, R. (2023, March 13). Does alternative grading make cheating more likely? *Grading for Growth*. https://gradingforgrowth.com/p/does-alternative-grading-make-cheating

Taylor, B., Kisby, F., & Reedy, A. (2024). Rubrics in higher education: An exploration of undergraduate students' understanding and perspectives. *Assessment & Evaluation in Higher Education, 49*(6), 799–809.

TED. (2012, March 22). *Talks by brilliant kids and teens* [Video playlist]. https://www.ted.com/playlists/129/ted_under_20

Tierney, J. (2013, January 9). Why teachers secretly hate grading papers. *The Atlantic*. https://www.theatlantic.com/national/archive/2013/01/why-teachers-secretly-hate-grading-papers/266931

Vatterott, C. (2015). *Rethinking grading: Meaningful assessment for standards-based learning*. ASCD.

Vygotsky, L. S. (1978). *Mind in society: The development of higher psychological processes*. Harvard University Press.

Watson, A. (2023, December 27). *Feedback before grades: Research and practice* Learning & the Brain. http://www.learningandthebrain.com/blog/feedback-before-grades-research-and-practice

Wilcox, G., Morett, L. M., Hawes, Z., & Dommett, E. J. (2021). Why educational neuroscience needs educational and school psychology to effectively translate neuroscience to educational practice. *Frontiers in Psychology, 11*, 618449.

Woolf, N. (2020, February 10). *What research says about giving effective feedback to students*. NovaEdu. https://insidesel.com/2020/02/10/researchbrief-feedback

Wormeli, R. (2006). *Fair isn't always equal: Assessing & grading in the differentiated classroom*. Stenhouse.

Wormeli, R. (2011). Redos and retakes done right. *Educational Leadership, 69*(3). https://www.ascd.org/el/articles/redos-and-retakes-done-right

Yoder, N., Ward, A. M., & Wolforth, S. (2021). *Teaching the whole child: Instructional practices that integrate equity-centered social, emotional, and academic learning*. American Institutes for Research. https://www.air.org/sites/default/files/2021-12/Social-Emotional-Learning-Equity-Centered-Instructional-Practices-December-2021.pdf

Zwiers, J., & Crawford, M. (2011). *Academic conversations: Classroom talk that fosters critical thinking and content understandings*. Stenhouse.

Index

Note: Page references followed by an italicized *f* indicates information contained in figures.

academic dishonesty, 8
accelerated learning, 56–57
accountability, 87, 104
active listening, 9
administrative support, 139–140
artificial intelligence (AI)
    and feedback, 34, 41–43
    for writing rubrics, 62
authenticity, 9, 139
autonomy, 106

biases
    in grading, 73, 121
    in single-shot assessment system, 83–84
book studies, 140–142
Brockback, Brennan, 30–31, 63
buy-in, 139

Carlsen, Jake, 129
check-ins, 13, 102–103
checklists, 102
classroom culture and routines
    feedback as part of, 43–45
    practice work and grading, 10–11
cognitive alliances with students, 35–36
collaborative assessment, 45–47
collaborative learning, 13–17
collegial collaboration, 56, 90–91, 95–96
Compton, Joel, 85
conferences, student-teacher, 37–41, 38*f*, 40*f*

connectedness to school, 107
culturally responsive feedback processes, 35
culturally responsive teaching, 145

Daley, Sara, 36, 76, 91–92
deadlines, flexible, 102–103, 108
decaying-average grading method, 125–126
departmental teams, 138–139
Dewey, John, 13
Díaz, Osvaldo, 137, 139
differentiated instruction, 65
digital divide, 43
digital grading systems, 119–121
disabilities, students with, 9
distance learning, 37
Doucette, Alex, 21, 88–89, 92, 96
Dweck, Carol, 83

effort grading, 116
empathy, 94
engagement. *See* student engagement and motivation
English-language learners, 100
equity gaps
    feedback and, 32, 39–41
    technology access, 43
expectations, high, 87, 94–95, 100
extension requests, 104–105
extrinsic motivation, 9

facilitator, 13
failing grades, 52–53
family engagement
    communication practices, 81–82
    data-driven approaches and, 25
    feedback on grading reform from, 25
    grade inflation *versus* high standards, 23–24
    grading and, 21–23
    parent-teacher conferences, 81
    and retake policies, 97
    rubrics implementation, 60–62
feedback
    benefits of using on formative tasks, 47–48
    and classroom culture, 43–45
    collaborative assessment, 45
    criteria for effective, 28–29, 35–37
    culture shift to accepting, 48–49
    flex days, makeup days, and review days, 36–37
    and goal-setting, 32–35, 33*f*, 37
    group, 30
    honing learning intentions, 37
    just-in-time feedback, 31–32
    mixing grades with, 27–28
    online breakout rooms, 37
    pause and reflect, 49–50
    peer assessment, 45–47
    and project-based learning, 102
    project-based learning and workshop model, 36
    purposeful and personalized, 35–37
    streamlining processes of, 29–35
    technologies to support, 41–43
    tracking feedback and progress, 37–41, 38*f*, 40*f*
feedback on grading reforms, 24–25
Feldman, Joe, 126
50 percent floor problems, 117
flex days, 36–37
flex periods, 108
formative feedback, 47–48
formative work. *See* practice work

gallery walks, 45
Ghassemi, LaRee, 106, 115
goal-setting
    and feedback, 32–35, 33*f*
    tracking feedback and progress, 37–41, 38*f*, 40*f*
grace periods, 105–106
gradebook, standards-based, 119–121, 119*f*–120*f*
grade inflation, 23–24
grades/grading. *See also* feedback; late-work policies; retakes; rubrics; schoolwide implementation of new grading practices
    collaborative practice, 126–128
    decaying-average grading method, 125–126
    digital grading systems, 119–121
    50 percent floor problems, 117
    100-point scale, 52–53
    hybrid systems, 115
    minimum-grade policies, 117
    mixing with feedback, 27–28
    most recent grading method, 123–124
    pitfalls of grading scales, 116
    point-based grading, 116
    prioritizing current understanding, 122–126
    process over grades, 11
    simplified and weighted-average grading, 121–122
    standards-based gradebook example, 119–121, 119*f*–120*f*
    standards-based grading, 112–113, 117–122, 119*f*–120*f*
    student-led progress tracking and, 79–80
    sustained progress grading method, 124–125
    transparency, 122
    zeros, 53, 116, 129
"Grading for Equity" (Feldman), 126
Green, Katie, 126–128
group work, 13–14
growth mindset, 44, 62, 83, 113

Haber, Kim, 9, 13, 16, 30, 62, 115
habits of mind, 15, 75, 113
Hammond, Zaretta, 85
higher-order thinking skills, 65
Holden, Katherine, 10, 55

holistic assessment, 123
homework
    as instructional tool, 30–31
    ungrading, 19–20, 20f
Hubbard, Michelle, 131–132, 142–143
100-point scale, 52–53, 116
The Hungry Mind: The Origins of Curiosity in Childhood (Engel), 25

Ickes, Rob, 16
instruction
    differentiated instruction, 65
    targeted teaching, 63–64
introverted students, 9

Jensen, Eric, 32
Johnson, Breanne, 101

kikan-shidō, 31
King, Tim, 107–108
Kleinfeld, Judith, 94–95

Larsen, Tim, 111, 126
late-work policies, 99
    benefits of constructive, 113–114
    check-ins, 103–104
    customizing support for students, 106–107
    extension requests, 104–105
    features of supportive, 104–106
    flexible deadlines and, 102–103
    focus on learning, 109–110
    grace periods, 105–106
    issues around formulating, 101
    pitfalls of punitive, 100
    poor-quality, 110–111
    project-based learning and, 102
    standards-based approach to, 107–108, 112–113
    summative assessments and, 109–110, 111–112
    work in progress submissions, 105
learning disabilities, students with, 100
learning management systems (LMSs)
    budget-driven decision making, 131–132
    constraints, 127–128, 129
    overcoming barriers, 132–135
    reporting challenges, 129–131, 130f
    reporting frequency requirements, 131
    selection criteria for, 133f–134f
    student and parent views, 130
Linklater, Katie, 16, 68–71, 129–130
Longnecker, Emily, 21, 31, 64
López, Sergio, 48, 93, 97

makeup days, 36–37
marginalized students
    bias in grading, 73
    rubrics and, 71
mastery emphasis, 123
mental health, 106–107
metacognition, 33, 87
minimum-grade policies, 117
most recent grading method, 123–124
motivation. *See* student engagement and motivation
multilingual learners and class participation grading, 9
multitiered systems of support (MTSS), 146
Mundorff, Laura, 17–19, 29

newsletters, family, 81

O'Brien, Conor, 109–110, 122, 137, 142
one-on-one support, 110
online breakout rooms, 37
ownership, 12, 29, 49, 52, 101

participation grades, 7, 9, 10–11, 18, 93, 116
peer assessment, 29, 45–48, 102
philosophical conflicts, 136–137
practice work
    benefits of feedback, 47–48
    classroom culture and routines, 10–11
    collaborative learning, 13–17
    data-driven approaches, 25
    family engagement, 21–25
    family feedback on, 25
    grade inflation, 23–24
    implementing change in, 15–16, 21
    as instructional tools, 30–31
    integrity issues, 8
    meaning and relevance, 12–13
    pause and reflect, 25–26
    pitfalls of grading, 7–8
    process over grades, 11
    scaffolding collaborative work, 14

skill strengthening, 13–14
spotlight on, 17–19
student engagement and motivation, 10–13, 14–17
student feedback on, 24–25
student stress, 8
and summative assessments, 109–110
teacher workload and priorities, 8
tuning into practice, 19
turning point in ungrading approach, 21
ungrading homework, 19–20, 20f
preparedness, 87
problem-solving, 65
process, importance of, 11
professional judgment, 123
professional learning committees (PLCs), 137–138
progress tracking
    feedback and, 37–41, 38f, 40f
    in project-based learning, 102
    student-led progress tracking, 77–79, 78f
project-based learning, 36, 102
protocols to support understanding, 14
punctuality *versus* content mastery, 100

Reafleng, John, 131
REAL criteria (readiness, endurance, assessed, leverage), 55–56
real-world application, 12, 23
reasoning, 65
reflection, 110
reluctant learners, and retakes, 94
reporter, 14
responsibility, 87
retakes, 83–84
    Assessment Retake Application Form, 85, 86f
    during class, 91
    collaborative study plans for, 85, 86f
    collegial collaboration for, 90–91, 95–96
    diagnosing first attempt issues, 84
    example implementation, 88–89
    family engagement, 97
    high expectations, 87, 94–95
    improve performance, 84–89, 86f
    as insurance policy for all students, 93–95
    oral option, 88–89
    pause and reflect, 97–98
    pinpointing learning gaps, 91–92
    and poor quality late work, 111
    practice work review, 85–87
    pre-assessment screening, 92–93
    requiring, 87
    and school schedules, 90
    streamlining implementation of, 89–93
    summative assessments and, 111–112
    supporting reluctant learners, 94
    time and number limits, 92–93
review days, 36–37
rote skills and procedures, 65
Rubistar, 62
rubrics
    advantages of, 53–54
    creation efficiency, 62–63
    criteria definition, 57–58
    design considerations, 54–58
    embedding across classroom experience, 68–71, 70f
    family engagement in process, 60–62
    and grades, 65–68, 66f–67f
    learning management systems and, 116
    phased implementation, 58–62, 59f, 60f–61f
    schoolwide systemic implementation benefits, 71–72
    as shared framework for learning, 64–65
    standards identification, 54–57
    and student collaboration, 72
    student involvement in creation, 52
    targeted teaching, 63–64

schoolwide implementation of new grading practices
    book studies and awareness, 140–142
    culturally responsive teaching, 145
    departmental teams, 138–139
    example change case, 142–143
    integrating other practices with, 144–145
    multitiered systems of support (MTSS), 146
    pause and reflect, 147
    professional learning committees, 137–138
    resolving philosophy conflicts, 136–137
    shifting professional mindset, 146–147
    social and emotional learning, 144–145

schoolwide implementation of new grading practices *(cont'd)*
  teacher leadership and administrative support, 139–140
  trauma-informed practices, 145
schoolwide implementation of rubrics, 71–72
schoolwide policies on retakes, 95–96
self-assessment, 18, 29, 43–44, 74–75, 102
self-esteem, 29
showcasing student thinking, 44
simplified grading, 121–122
single-point rubrics, 58, 59*f*, 60*f*–61*f*
single-shot assessment, 83
small group support, 110
social and emotional learning, 10, 144–145
standard-by-standard evaluation, 123
standardized testing, 12
standards
  grade inflation *versus* high, 23–24
  rubrics and, 54–57
standards-based approach to late work, 107–108
standards-based grading, 112–113, 117–122, 119*f*–120*f*
Status of the Class document, 37, 38*f*
Stegner, Collin, 19, 45–46
stress, 8, 106–107
student-centered evaluation practices
  benefits, 74–75
  collaboration on rubrics and assessment, 72
  pitfalls of teacher-centric recordkeeping, 72–74
  student-led progress tracking, 77–79, 78*f*
  student reflection and goal setting, 75–77
student engagement and motivation, 7, 9
  classroom culture and routines, 10–11
  collaborative learning and, 14–17
  feedback and, 27–28
  meaningful and relevant practice, 12–13
  process over grades, 11
  self-assessment and, 74
student-friendly language, 57
student-led progress tracking, 79–80
student management systems (SMSs), 129

students
  choice, 12, 20, 102
  cognitive alliances with, 35–36
  feedback on grading reforms, 24–25
  habits of mind, 15, 75, 85, 113
  stress, 8, 106–107
student spotlight, 44
study habits, 85
summative assessments
  overreliance on, 73
  practice work on, 109–110
  retakes, 111–112
  student trackers and, 79–80
  ungraded practice work and, 22
sustainability, 139
sustained progress grading method, 124–125

teacher-centric recordkeeping, 72–74
teacher education, 68
teacher-led reform, 139–140
team work, 13–14
technology. *See also* learning management systems (LMSs)
  and feedback, 34, 41–43
  rubrics, 62
test tracking sheets, 77
Thelan, Dylan, 30
timekeeper, 13
time management skills, 102–104, 106
transparency in grading, 51–52, 73–74
trauma-informed practices, 69, 145

Veto, Rachel, 19–20, 32–35, 33*f*, 55

warm demander role, 94–95
weighted-average grading, 118, 121–122
work in progress submission policies, 105
workload and priorities, 8, 29–35, 89–93, 138
workshop model, 36
written reflections, 9
Wyckoff, Isaiah, 75, 113, 126

Yang, Shuang, 84, 87

zeros, 53, 116, 129
zone of proximal development, 35–36

About the Authors

Howard Yank, faculty emeritus at Portland State University's College of Education, brings more than 25 years of secondary teaching experience across California, Oregon, Washington, and international schools in Latin America. He earned his bachelor's degree from the University of California, Berkeley, and holds a master's in history from San Francisco State University. From the outset of his career, Howard has been committed to social justice and inquiry-based learning.

He pioneered and taught in a dual-language Spanish secondary program in Eugene, Oregon, and played a pivotal role in establishing similar programs in Vancouver Public Schools, Washington. As a curriculum administrator, instructional coach, and teacher mentor, Howard has advanced equitable practices in schools throughout the United States and Mexico. In addition to his work at Portland State University, Howard has also trained teachers at La Universidad Autónoma Benito Juárez de Oaxaca, the University of Oregon, and Washington State University, Vancouver.

Internationally, Howard taught in Mexico, Costa Rica, and Chile, gaining specialized expertise in International Baccalaureate diploma programs. His articles have appeared in the Feminist Press, *NEA Today, California Monthly, Oregon Education,* and ASCD. As an equity grading coach, Howard supports teachers nationwide and remains deeply involved in professional development, mentoring, and equity-driven initiatives.

Howard can be reached at hyank@pdx.edu.

 **Maika Yeigh** is an associate professor in the Graduate School of Education & Counseling at Lewis & Clark College, where she works with teacher candidates seeking initial licensure. Many passions feed her work as a teacher educator: preparing teachers who are ready to meet the needs of learners, improving clinical preparation practices for novice teachers, and supporting teachers as they develop and implement humane assessment practices. She believes that strong practitioner research relies on creating connections to local classrooms and the work that teachers do on a daily basis. Maika spent the beginning of her career teaching middle school and high school and has also worked as a reading specialist in the elementary setting. She spends time building and maintaining relationships with teachers, administrators, and other school stakeholders. She is also the managing editor of the *Northwest Journal of Teacher Education*, is the president of the Oregon Association of Teacher Education, and has published articles in regional and national journals.

Related Resources

ASCD Books is an imprint of ISTE+ASCD, whose mission is to empower educators to reimagine and redesign learning through impactful pedagogy and meaningful technology use. We achieve this by offering transformative professional learning, cultivating and disseminating thought leadership, fostering vibrant communities, and ensuring that digital tools and experiences are accessible and effective.

At the time of publication, the following resources related to this book's topic were available:

Amplify Student Voices: Equitable Practices to Build Confidence in the Classroom by AnnMarie Baines, Diana Medina, and Caitlin Healy (ASCD Book)

Equity in Data: A Framework for What Counts in Schools by Andrew Knips, Sonya Lopez, Michael Savoy, and Kendall LaParo (ASCD Book)

Giving Students a Say: Smarter Assessment Practices to Empower and Engage by Myron Dueck (ASCD Book)

Grading for Student Learning by Susan M. Brookhart (Quick Reference Guide)

Grading Smarter, Not Harder: Assessment Strategies That Motivate Kids and Help Them Learn by Myron Dueck (ASCD Book)

Questioning for Formative Feedback: Meaningful Dialogue to Improve Learning by Jackie Acree Walsh (ASCD Book)

Meaningful Classroom Management: Adapting Your Teaching to Build Culture and Community by Sheldon L. Eakins (ASCD Book)

Rethinking Grading: Meaningful Assessment for Standards-Based Learning by Cathy Vatterott (ASCD Book)

Rethinking Homework: Best Practices That Support Diverse Needs (2nd Ed.) by Cathy Vatterott (ASCD Book)

Student-Led Assessment: Promoting Agency and Achievement Through Portfolios and Conferences by Starr Sackstein (ASCD Book)

What We Know About Grading: What Works, What Doesn't, and What's Next by Thomas R. Guskey and Susan M. Brookhart (ASCD Book)

For up-to-date information about ISTE+ASCD resources, go to www.iste-ascd.org/books-and-publications. To learn more about membership and join or renew, go to www.iste-ascd.org/membership, email memsupport@iste-ascd.org, or call 1-800-933-2723 or 703-578-9600.

An ASCD Study Guide for *Equitable Grading Unlocked: Practical Strategies from the Classroom*

This ASCD Study Guide is designed to enhance your understanding and application of the information contained in *Equitable Grading Unlocked: Practical Strategies from the Classroom*, an ASCD book written by Howard Yank and Maika Yeigh, published in January 2026. You can use the study guide after you have read the book or as you finish each chapter. The study questions provided are not meant to cover all aspects of the book but, rather, to address specific ideas that might warrant further reflection. Many of the questions and activities in this study guide can be explored individually. However, this guide is specifically designed to support book study groups of educators who read, discuss, reflect on, and experiment with the book's ideas together as they consider how to implement or apply them.

When forming a book study group, teachers might team up with colleagues from their professional learning community (PLC), grade-level or department teams, or others with similar roles or interest in the book. In schools where such structures are limited—or for teachers who teach unique or singleton courses—participants can connect across schools or districts with peers who share similar assignments or curiosity. This flexible approach ensures that all educators, regardless of context, can find a supportive group for rich discussion and collaborative learning.

When engaging in a book study group, we recommend these steps to establish a positive and productive environment:

1. Set Group Norms and Agreements: Begin by collaboratively establishing expectations for active listening, respectful dialogue, confidentiality, and equitable participation so all voices are valued.
2. Define the Pace of Reading: Agree on how much to read between meetings, such as completing a chapter each session, to maintain steady progress together. Decide on a session schedule, whether weekly, biweekly, or monthly, to maintain continuity and momentum.
3. Establish Reflection and Application Guidelines: Given the questions and activities suggested for each chapter, decide how members will reflect on and pilot recommended strategies in their classrooms, encouraging thoughtful experimentation.

4. Check in Regularly: At each meeting, take time to revisit group norms, discuss what's working, and adjust expectations as needed to keep engagement high.

By following these steps, study groups can create a supportive atmosphere that maximizes professional learning and collaboration. At the initial meeting, consider appointing or inviting a volunteer facilitator to help organize logistics, keep discussions focused, and ensure that the group stays on track with its reading and implementation goals. The facilitator's role is not to act as an "expert" but as a supportive guide who encourages broad engagement, manages group agreements, and helps synthesize takeaways.

As you progress through the book, set aside time during each meeting for members to share reflections, raise questions, and discuss strategies they've piloted and practical ways to apply new ideas. The goal is to create a collaborative environment for experimentation, professional growth, and support as each participant explores equitable grading practices in their own context. As your group implements and refines strategies, consider sharing pilot findings and insights with colleagues beyond your study group—through informal conversations, staff meetings, or schoolwide presentations—to encourage broader dialogue and ongoing learning within your school community.

Introduction

Choose two or three prompts from the following questions to respond to and discuss with your book study group (or with a colleague).

1. What challenges or dilemmas about equitable grading practices did you find most relatable or thought provoking in the introduction?
2. In what ways does the introduction connect with your own experiences or observations around grading, motivation, or student engagement? How do the voices of teachers included here contribute to your interest in learning more?
3. How does the introduction's focus on practical strategies and real classroom examples shape your expectations for what you'll find in the rest of the book?

4. In what ways does the introduction motivate you, as an educator, a coach, or an administrator, to dive deeper into grading reform or sustain engagement through the book study? How does this resonate with your goals for professional growth or school culture?

Chapter 1: Practice Work

Choose two or three prompts from each section to respond to, discuss, or act upon with your book study group (or with a colleague).

Reflective Questions

1. Which stories or research in this chapter most challenged your own assumptions about grading practice work? What specific questions did they raise for your context?
2. How do you currently balance student accountability with fostering intrinsic motivation? What shifts might you consider after engaging with this chapter's ideas?
3. What approaches could you use to increase authentic engagement among students without relying on grades or other external rewards?
4. What challenges do you foresee in communicating the value of ungraded practice work to students, families, or colleagues? How might you address these?
5. Reflect on a time when grading practice work either supported or undermined learning in your context. What's one of the things you would do differently now?

Extension and Pilot Suggestions

1. Identify a routine task, assignment, or activity that could be transformed into ungraded practice. What outcomes might you anticipate for learners?
2. Experiment with incorporating more opportunities for self-reflection or self-assessment, as described in this chapter, and note any effects on motivation or achievement.
3. Analyze relevant data—such as completion rates, growth metrics, assessment results, or student survey results—to demonstrate the impact of practice work in your role to students, families, or colleagues.

4. Pilot a collaborative initiative to co-create practice work norms or routines with students or colleagues. Document the process and outcomes.
5. Consider what resources, supports, or changes would help you, your team, or your school successfully implement ungraded practice work. Then take one step to access or advocate for them.

Chapter 2: Grades Versus Feedback

<u>Circling Back</u>

Before focusing on this chapter, book study participants should briefly share whether they have begun to implement any strategies from the previous chapter. Describe both successes and challenges, so the group can discuss refinements and support one another's efforts.

Choose two or three prompts from each of the sections below to respond to, discuss, or act upon with your book study group (or with a colleague).

<u>Reflective Questions</u>

1. The teachers in this chapter shared their discomfort when students hyper-focused on grades over learning. Which of the teacher's stories were most familiar for you?
2. What are some ways you could shift your in-class time to provide opportunities for students to read, understand, and implement the feedback you provide?
3. In what places do your students have ownership of their learning in your classroom? What are some additional ways to provide more opportunities for students to take ownership?
4. What trends do you commonly see in your students' work that could be addressed in whole-class instruction as a step in the revision process similar to the strategy that Dylan used?
5. In what ways do your department or PLC work together to align grading structures? What are some additional opportunities for collaboration?

<u>Extension and Pilot Suggestions</u>

1. Choose an upcoming formative assessment on which to provide actionable feedback, including time for students to process and implement the feedback.

2. Consider practice work that would benefit from peers providing feedback to one another. Teach students the compliment-question feedback strategy, and have them practice it with the chosen practice work.
3. For an upcoming project, multistep assignment, or other structured workday, try taking a Status of the Class to both encourage self-reflection and time management.
4. In the "Creating a Culture Shift" section (pp. 48–49), it is noted that making these changes takes time and persistence. Review the stepping-stones described in this chapter and choose one to try. What data could you use to see if it is producing the outcomes you were hoping for?

Chapter 3: Rubrics and Progress Tracking

<u>Circling Back</u>

Before focusing on this chapter, book study participants should briefly share whether they have begun to implement any strategies from the previous chapter. Describe both successes and challenges, so the group can discuss refinements and support one another's efforts.

Choose two or three prompts from each of the sections below to respond to, discuss, or act upon with your book study group (or with a colleague).

<u>Reflective Questions</u>

1. When have you or your colleagues observed a disconnect between students' sense of their own preparedness and actual performance on assessments? What factors contributed to this gap? How could clearer criteria have changed the outcome?
2. How transparent are your current grading practices for students and families? In what ways might greater transparency promote more equitable outcomes?
3. In your experience, how does the use of rubrics (or lack thereof) influence student motivation, ownership, and engagement with learning? Can you recall an instance where a rubric helped—or hindered—student progress?
4. What challenges have you faced in identifying and focusing on true "essential standards" for your subject or grade level? How have you worked through these challenges with your team or students?

5. How do you see the balance between teacher- and student-led progress monitoring playing out in your context? What are the potential benefits and pitfalls of shifting more responsibility for tracking learning to students themselves?

Extension and Pilot Suggestions

1. Pilot integrating a student-friendly rubric into an upcoming assignment or assessment. Invite students to use the rubric for self-assessment before submitting their work, and gather feedback on their experience.
2. With your grade-level, subject, or professional learning community team, collaboratively identify a limited set of essential standards to feature in an upcoming unit, and co-design rubrics that clearly articulate criteria and performance levels.
3. Try embedding rubric criteria directly into assessment tasks or projects so students can connect their work to expectations in real time. Reflect with students on whether this changes how they approach or understand the assignment.
4. Implement a (digital or hard copy) student progress tracker and support students in recording their own performance after assessments. Collect insights on how this influences their goal setting and sense of ownership over learning.
5. Choose one area of classroom or schoolwide practice (e.g., communication with families, behavioral expectations, peer feedback) and adapt or design a rubric to clarify expectations. Use this tool as a basis for discussion with students, families, or colleagues, and adjust your approach based on their input.

Chapter 4: Redos and Retakes Done Right

Circling Back

Before focusing on this chapter, book study participants should briefly share whether they have begun to implement any strategies from the previous chapter. Describe both successes and challenges, so the group can discuss refinements and support one another's efforts.

Choose two or three prompts from each of the sections below to respond to, discuss, or act upon with your book study group (or with a colleague).

Reflective Questions

1. In this chapter, offering redos and retakes is connected to the concept of a growth mindset. Describe a policy or structure—other than retakes—that you have found effective for supporting persistence and mastery in students. What are the pros and cons relative to redos?
2. When a student doesn't do well on an assessment, can you usually tell why that happened? If not, what ideas do you have for finding out?
3. Consider Sara Daley's in-class "target table days." What logistics would you want to have in place prior to offering a similar opportunity for your students?
4. What grading practice could you eliminate or streamline that would allow you time to offer redos to your students?
5. As you make shifts to your grading policies, what will parents and other caregivers need to know in order to support both you and their children?

Extension and Pilot Suggestions

1. Choose an upcoming assessment and allow students to retake the parts of the assessment in which they do poorly. Consider what you will want them to do to prepare for the retake so they get a different outcome, including using a retake application form.
2. Begin with one assessment on which most students have demonstrated success. Offer an oral retake option for students who are struggling to articulate their learning through writing.
3. Consider working with your PLC, department, or any other colleagues who want to partner with you to provide retake opportunities for students during the school day. Each teacher could take one shift to share the load.
4. When you try a new grading strategy, prepare parents by crafting communication in a way that explains the change and emphasizes that you care about their children and their children's learning.
5. What data would you want to collect before and after implementing retakes or redos to evaluate its success? Consider sharing these data with students, colleagues, and families.

Chapter 5: Untimely and Unfinished

Circling Back

Before focusing on this chapter, book study participants should briefly share whether they have begun to implement any strategies from the previous chapter. Describe both successes and challenges, so the group can discuss refinements and support one another's efforts.

Choose two or three prompts from each of the sections below to respond to, discuss, or act upon with your book study group (or with a colleague).

Reflective Questions

1. What aspects of your current late-work policy could you modify to better support student learning? Which elements might be easy or challenging to agree upon if developing a shared policy with other teachers?
2. How can you intentionally combine the importance of meeting deadlines with the flexibility some students may need to be successful in your classroom?
3. Which are the most meaningful assignments that you provide to students? Are there assignments that are less important and could be eliminated?
4. Are there ways that students could make use of their practice work on summative assessments within your classroom? What would you need to modify for that to be effective?
5. Which unit that you currently teach could benefit from incorporating a project-based learning opportunity? How could that project provide you with options to try out strategies to keep students on track with their work?

Extension and Pilot Suggestions

1. On an upcoming assignment, provide an "optimum" due date and a "flexible" due date. Support students toward meeting the optimum date through check-ins and progress trackers. At the end, look at the data to see how many students met the optimum date.
2. Talk with your PLC, department, or grade-level team about developing a consistent late-work policy. Consider using the unified late-work policy explained by Tim King in the Spotlight section (pp. 107–108), which allows students to turn in work until the end of the unit.

3. Choose one assignment that has a handful of late submissions of poor quality. Try the scaffolds found in this chapter (e.g., reflection, one-on-one support with feedback, resubmission) with a relatively short resubmission window. Do you see improvements to student learning as a result?
4. In an upcoming unit, ask students to maintain their practice work so they can reference it during the final assessment or beyond. Do you notice any differences in how students interact with their practice work?

Chapter 6: Upgrading Your Gradebook

Circling Back

Before focusing on this chapter, book study participants should briefly share whether they have begun to implement any strategies from the previous chapter. Describe both successes and challenges, so the group can discuss refinements and support one another's efforts.

Choose two or three prompts from each of the sections below to respond to, discuss, or act upon with your book study group (or with a colleague).

Reflective Questions

1. In what ways do your current gradebook and grading practices reflect—or distort—actual student learning? How might shifting the focus affect your students?
2. Reflect on your school's or district's use of traditional grading scales (percentage/points-based). How have these systems influenced motivation, equity, or communication with students and families?
3. What challenges have you or your colleagues encountered when aligning grading practices with standards-based principles, especially within the constraints of your school's LMS or reporting software?
4. How does the culture of teacher autonomy or resistance to change at your site affect efforts to implement more transparent and equitable grading practices?
5. Considering the different grading methods described in this chapter (e.g., most recent, sustained progress, decaying average). Which approach most aligns with your subject area, and what questions or concerns would you want to explore as a team?

<u>Extension and Pilot Suggestions</u>

1. Choose an upcoming unit or grading period to pilot organizing your gradebook by essential standards or learning objectives, replacing traditional categories with rubric-based scoring.
2. Collaborate with colleagues or your team to analyze your current gradebook set-up, and identify at least one change you could make to increase grading accuracy and equity (e.g., reducing weighted categories, minimizing punitive practices).
3. Experiment with either the most recent, sustained progress, or decaying average grading method for a set of assessments. Record your observations on how this influences student engagement, understanding, and reported grades.
4. Communicate with students and families about a new approach to grading or reporting, such as introducing standards-based progress reports or sharing conversion charts. Gather feedback and adjust your communication strategy based on what you learn.
5. If you use digital gradebooks or LMS systems, explore their customization options (or suggest alternatives to leadership) to better align grade reporting with equitable assessment. Consider joining or forming a committee to advocate for more supportive technology choices.

Chapter 7: Schoolwide Implementation of New Grading Practices

<u>Circling Back</u>

Before focusing on this chapter, book study participants should briefly share whether they have begun to implement any strategies from the previous chapter. Describe both successes and challenges, so the group can discuss refinements and support one another's efforts.

Choose two or three prompts from each of the sections below to respond to, discuss, or act upon with your book study group (or with a colleague).

<u>Reflective Questions</u>

1. How have differences in grading policies among colleagues influenced student perceptions of fairness, motivation, or confusion at your school?

2. Reflecting on your experiences with professional learning communities (PLCs) or departmental teams, what factors have helped or hindered collaborative efforts to align grading practices?
3. In what ways has teacher leadership or administrative support (or their absence) affected progress toward equitable grading reforms in your context?
4. How might integrating equitable grading with existing practices (such as SEL, trauma-informed approaches, or culturally responsive teaching) deepen impact for all students?
5. As your school or district works toward more coherent grading practices, what mindsets or beliefs about assessment and student success might need to shift among staff or leadership?

Extension and Pilot Suggestions

1. With colleagues, co-design and implement a shared grading protocol or specific strategy (such as a common rubric or reassessment guideline) across several classrooms or subjects. Then bring comparative student outcomes and feedback to the group for analysis and refinement.
2. Instead of piloting a classroom-based strategy, collaboratively engage your book study group in planning and hosting an informational session or workshop for families, students, or other staff. Use this forum to share your group's emerging practices, address common questions, and solicit feedback from broader school community stakeholders—helping foster transparency, buy-in, and deeper engagement with equity grading reforms.
3. Collaborate with colleagues to develop communication tools (e.g., newsletters, parent guides, information sessions) that clarify new grading practices and share the rationale and observed benefits with families and school stakeholders.
4. Consider how your current grading system intersects with SEL, MTSS, or culturally responsive practices, and select one area where you can intentionally link grading reforms with broader initiatives for student support.
5. Using your group's collective learnings and experience, create a presentation, resource guide, or professional development session that shares your implementation journey—and insights—with a wider school or district audience, aiming to inspire or support systemic change.

Moving Forward

As emphasized in the opening pages of *Equitable Grading Unlocked*, details in grading practices matter deeply—and attending to them can make the work both challenging and worthwhile. Nearly every teacher featured in this book began with small, incremental shifts, focusing on a single change and refining it before moving forward with the next. We encourage you to approach grading reform in your classroom, school, or district with the same intentional, step-by-step mindset. Seek out like-minded colleagues—whether in your PLC, department, or wider professional network—so you can share ideas, experiment together, and support one another's progress.

Some teachers in this book formed collaborative teams to design new systems and pilot strategies collectively; others took the first steps alone, reaching out to broader networks for guidance and encouragement. At the core of this work is a shared commitment to do better for students: to help them see their own potential and to remove barriers to meaningful learning. Grading practices wield enormous power; they can either empower or discourage. For example, a 9th grader failing just one class is at greater risk of not graduating. This reality makes it our critical responsibility to ensure that our grading aligns with learning and supports every student in an equitable way.

We hope you find your allies in this journey, discover ways to let go of practices that steal time from meaningful instruction, and witness your students growing—motivated by the intrinsic rewards of learning itself.

DON'T MISS A SINGLE ISSUE OF THIS AWARD-WINNING MAGAZINE.

iste+ascd
educational leadership

If you belong to a Professional Learning Community, you may be looking for a way to get your fellow educators' minds around a complex topic. Why not delve into a relevant theme issue of *Educational Leadership*, the journal written by educators for educators?

Subscribe now and browse or purchase back issues of our flagship publication at **www.ascd.org/el**. Discounts on bulk purchases are available.

iste+ascd

Arlington, VA USA
1-800-933-2723

www.ascd.org
www.iste.org